Presented to

.....Laurateen Renae Ford....

From

.....Mom + Dad............

Date

.....June 15, 1997..........

DEAR GRADUATE

LETTERS OF WISDOM
FROM
Charles Swindoll

WORD PUBLISHING
Dallas • London • Vancouver • Melbourne

All text originally appeared in *Living Above the
Level of Mediocrity* by Charles R. Swindoll.
© by Charles R. Swindoll 1987, 1989.

J. Countryman is a registered trademark of
Word Publishing, Inc.

A J. Countryman Book

*Designed by Koechel Peterson & Associates, Inc.,
Minneapolis, Minnesota.*

Edited by Terri Gibbs

ISBN: 0-8499-5237-9

Printed and bound in the United States of America

7 8 9 Q P F   9 8 7 6 5 4 3

TABLE OF CONTENTS

*G*raduation marks an ending and a beginning. There are smiles, hugs, tears, shouts of joy, and caps sailing high into the air along with hopes and dreams. It is a time of celebration, excitement, and full-throttle enthusiasm.

Great word, *enthusiasm*. Its Greek origin is *entheos*, "God in." It is the ability to see God in a situation that makes it exciting. Do you know that God is watching your life? Do you realize that? Something happens to us when we become convinced that God our heavenly Father is aware of and involved in our activities and is, in fact, applauding our lives.

Think of all you have accomplished to this point. Try to imagine the horizons and challenges of your future. As you mentally travel from the vanishing point of yesterday to the vanishing point of tomorrow you will find that God has been and always will be present. There is not a place in the entire scope of your existence where God is not there. There is purpose, there is meaning in the presence of God. Even in the things we may consider pointless, insignificant, trivial, or boring. Talk about an exciting thought!

Today may be the first day you realized that your heavenly Father is watching you in life. He is not absent, unconcerned, blind, deaf, or dead. He is watching because He cares. That can make all the difference in the world. Especially in a world where mediocrity calls the cadence . . . where quality and integrity and authenticity are negotiables.

Call me a dreamer, but I'm convinced that achieving one's full potential is still a goal worth striving for—that excellence is still worth pursuing even if most yawn and a few sneer. While there may not be millions out there who think like this, there are still a few . . . a very important few. You are probably among them.

Therefore, as you graduate, I'd like to challenge you to follow God's best. More specifically, to live a "God-enthused" life. That's the purpose of these letters. They come from my heart to yours. I am excited for you, because I have unlimited expectations for your life—and, more importantly, unwavering faith in the One who can accomplish them.

CHUCK SWINDOLL

PRIORITIES

LETTER NUMBER 1

Life is a lot like a coin; you can spend it any way you wish, but you can spend it only once. Choosing one thing over all the rest throughout life is a difficult thing to do. This is especially true when the choices are so many and the possibilities are so close.

To be completely truthful with you, however, we aren't left with numerous possibilities. Jesus Himself gave us the top priority:

"But seek first His kingdom and His righteousness; and all these things shall be added to you" (Matt. 6:33).

He said, in effect, "This is your priority; this comes first."

If I am to seek first in my life God's kingdom and God's righteousness, then whatever else I do ought to relate to that goal: where I work, with whom I spend my time, the one I marry, or the decision to remain single. Every decision I make ought to be filtered through the Matthew 6:33 filter: where I put my money, where and how I spend my time, what I buy, what I sell, what I give away.

Living out the kingdom life means that everything must remain before the throne and under the authority of the ruler. Everything must be held loosely.

What tangibles are you holding onto? What are you gripping tightly? Have they become your security? Are you a slave to some image? Some name you're trying to live up to?

Some job? Some possession? Some person?
Let me give you a tip. If you cannot let it go,
it's a priority to you. It is impossible to be a
slave to things or people and at the same time
be a faithful servant of God.

Life places before us hundreds of
possibilities. Some are bad. Many are good.
A few, the best. But each of us must decide,
"What is my choice? What is my reason
for living?" In other words, "What priority
takes first place in my life?"

Chuck Swindoll

ETHICS

LETTER NUMBER

*We need heroes.
I mean genuine heroes,
authentic men and women
who are admired for their
achievements, noble qualities,
and courage. Such people
aren't afraid to be different.
They risk. They stand
a cut above.*

Yet they are real human beings with flaws and failures like anyone else. But they inspire us to do better. We feel warm inside when we think about this rare breed of humanity. The kind we can look up to without the slightest suspicion of deception or hypocrisy. The kind who model excellence when no one is looking or for that matter when half the world is looking.

I'm concerned that we seem to be running shy of folks like that. Certainly, there are some, but not nearly as many, it seems, as when I was a small boy. Back then I distinctly recall looking up to numerous people in various segments of society—politics, athletics, education, science, the military, music, religion, aviation—all of whom not only stood tall during their heyday, but they finished well. Society mourned their passing. This was no childhood fantasy, you understand; these were not make-believe matinee idols. I can still remember my dad being just as impressed as I was with certain folks—maybe more so. Some of our father–son conversations are still logged in my memory bank. And because he was inspired, so was I.

You may be surprised to know that for any number of people, you are the person others

point to. It may be in the place where you work,
and no one has even told you. It may happen
where you live, and no neighbor has been brave
enough to encourage you by saying, "You're the
one everybody watches. You're very unique.
We all respect you." It may be in your school
where you are admired by colleagues and peers.
If you knew how many felt that way, I'm
convinced you would be all the more careful
how you live.

I am certain of this—if you are one of
those people, then you're not like the majority.
You're living differently, and I commend you for
it. It takes unusual people to make a difference
in our world. Mediocre people impact no one,
at least not for good. But one person of truth
can impact the whole world!

Chuck Swindoll

INTEGRITY

LETTER NUMBER

If some corporate position is the god of your life, then something terrible occurs within when it is no longer a future possibility. If your career, however, is simply a part of God's plan and you keep it in proper perspective, you can handle a demotion just as well as you can handle a promotion.

It all depends on who's first and what's first.

Breaking the magnet that draws things ahead of God is a lengthy and sometimes painful process. There is a line found in the Jewish Talmud that puts it well: "Man is born with his hands clenched; he dies with them wide open. Entering life, he desires to grasp everything; leaving the world, all he possessed has slipped away."

Everything created was through Christ and His power, and furthermore, it was created for His honor. That includes everyday things today. If you have a good job, it's to be enjoyed for Him. If you have a nice salary, it's to be enjoyed and invested for Him. Do you have good health? It is for Him. Are you planning a move? It's to be for Him. You're thinking about a career change? It needs to be for Him. That is true because He's the ruler of our kingdom. He is Lord.

You're dating a young man. You think you're falling in love with this man. Does Christ have first place in that relationship? Or have you decided that a moral compromise really feels better? Maybe you have chosen not to maintain such a strict standard of purity as before. If you've made that priority decision, then face it—Christ really isn't in first place in that romance.

Are you struggling right now between a decision that requires doing what is exactly right and losing closeness with an individual or giving in a little and keeping that friendship? You know the rest of the story. If Christ is going to have top priority, it must be according to the standard of His righteousness.

Just remember: Whatever is in first place, if it isn't Christ alone, it is in the wrong place.

Chuck Swindoll

Never take
your cues
from the crowd.

FLEXIBILITY

LETTER NUMBER

Are you open to change?
People who make a
difference can be stretched,
pulled, pushed, and changed.
You heard it from me:
Traditionalism is an old
dragon, bad about squeezing
the very life out of its
victims. So never stop
fighting it.

Let's be careful to identify the right opponent. It isn't tradition per se; it's traditionalism. I'm not trying to be petty, only accurate. The right kind of traditions give us deep roots—a solid network of reliable truth in a day when everything seems up for grabs. Among such traditions are those strong statements and principles that tie us to the mast of truth when storms of uncertainty create frightening waves of change driven by winds of doubt. For example: believing in the authority of holy Scripture, knowing and loving God, bowing to the Lordship of Jesus Christ, committing ourselves to others, and becoming people of genuine encouragement. Such traditions (there are others, of course) are valuable absolutes that keep us from feeling awash in a world of relativism and uncertainty.

However, there is a great deal of difference between tradition and traditionalism. By traditionalism, I have in mind mainly an attitude that resists change, adaptation, or alteration. It is holding fast to a custom or behavior that is being blindly and forcefully maintained. It is being suspicious of the new, the up-to-date, the different. It is finding one's

security, even identity, in the familiar and
therefore opposing whatever threatens that.
And if you'll allow me one more, it is substituting
a legalistic system for the freedom and freshness
of the Spirit—being more concerned about
keeping rigid, manmade rules than being
flexible, open to creativity and innovation.

By now you've guessed where I stand.
Clearly, my position is on the side of openness,
allowing room for the untried, the unpredictable,
the unexpected—all the while holding fast to the
truth. Believe me, there are plenty of people
around who feel it is their calling to tell
others what to do and what to say. They are
self-appointed wing-clippers who frown on
new ways and put down high flight. They
work hard to "squeeze you into their mold."

Whoever decides to soar must first fight
through the flatland fog that hangs heavy over
the swamp of sameness.

Chuck Swindoll

LETTER NUMBER

*Vision—the one essential
ingredient for being an
original in a day of copies
gets lost, overwhelmed
by the odds. Too bad!
We start focusing on the
trouble. Then we start
comparing the odds.*

The result is predictable: We become intimidated and wind up *defeated*.

What is your challenge? Which giants make you feel like a grasshopper when you face them? What does your future resemble when you measure it on the basis of facts and figures? You'd like not to surrender, right? You'd like to be courageous, wouldn't you? There is a way through, but you'll need one essential quality— *vision*.

Vision is the ability to see God's presence, to perceive God's power, to focus on God's plan in spite of the obstacles.

When you have vision it affects your attitude. Your attitude is optimistic rather than pessimistic. Your attitude stays positive rather than negative. Not foolishly positive, as though in fantasy, for you are reading God into your circumstances. So when a situation comes that cuts your feet out from under you, you don't throw up your arms and panic. You don't give up. Instead, you say, "Lord, this is Your moment. This is where You take charge. You're in this."

This is nothing more than having a strong belief in the power of God; having confidence in others around you who are in similar battles with you; and, yes, having confidence in yourself, by the grace of God. Refusing to give in to temptation, cynicism, and doubt. Not allowing yourself to become a jaded individual. Belief in oneself is terribly important.

Determination is hanging tough when the going gets rough. I have no magic wand to wave over your future and say, "All of a sudden everything is going to fall into place." Vision requires determination, a constant focus on God who is watching and smiling. Even in a world that is negative and hostile. Even in a world where the majority says, "We can't," you can. Trust God today. With eyes of faith, get back in the game. Play it with great enthusiasm!

Chuck Swindoll

COMMITMENT

LETTER NUMBER

People of excellence are those who see through the clutching greed of our times—people who have declared their undivided allegiance to Christ's message, people who have humbled themselves to Christ's sovereign authority.

If you are greatly gifted, you may be able to do marvelous things that would cause the public to be swept up in your skills and in your abilities. In the process of your growing, you will find great temptation to make a name for yourself, to make a big splash, to gain attention, to get the glory, to strut around, to increase your fees, to demand your rights, and to expect kid-glove treatment. You're in authority now! People are talking about you!

Let me remind you that if you're in life only for yourself, you'll have no endurance. On that precarious top of the ladder, you'll always have to maintain your balance by maneuvering and manipulating, lying, deceiving, and scheming. But if you're committed to kingdom-related excellence, when you go through times of testing, you can count on kingdom endurance to get you through.

If you're the kind of Christian who really wants the whole purpose of God, then you dare not leave out kingdom commitment. That means your motives must be investigated. For example, every time you make plans to acquire a sizable possession—a car, an expensive boat, a house, and such like—you must deal with it before God and ask: Is this His will? Would this honor Him? Would this glorify Him?

Am I suggesting that you take a vow of poverty? No, not that. My message is not that you go hungry and give up all nice things. I just say you give up control of them. Give all you have to the Lord God and trust Him to give back all that you need.

Chuck Swindoll

Excellence—
moral, ethical, personal
excellence—is
worth whatever
it costs.

CREATIVITY

LETTER NUMBER

God is a God of freshness and change. But wait, before I leave that thought, let me make something very clear: God Himself isn't changing, nor is His Son. He "is the same yesterday and today, yes and forever" (Heb. 13:8). Isn't that a great thought?

God is no different this year than He was last year or a decade ago. Nor will He change one hundred years from now. But even though He is the same, His working is different. It stays fresh. His ways and methods are forever fresh, unpredictably new.

I need to warn you, if you like things to stay the same, you're going to be terribly uncomfortable in heaven. Everything is going to be new. God is a God of freshness and change. He flexes His methods. He alters His way so much, it's as if you've never seen it before. You can't imagine what it may be like next time.

God says we are to be "imitators" of Him, which really means we are to "mimic." Since God is a God of freshness and change, so we should be. If we are to fulfill this command, then I suggest that we stay fresh—that we remain open, innovative, willing to change.

Every age knows the temptation to try to restrict God's dealings. The majority of people in this world are maintainers. Once we get things set, we don't like them changed.

Are you open to change in your life? Are you willing to risk? Are you flexible enough to innovate? Are you willing to tolerate the sheer possibility of making a massive change in your direction for life? "Lord, is it South America? Great! Or Indonesia? I'll do it. I'll move or change my profession. Fine! Are You leading me into a new venture? I'll do it. Count me in!"

That's the spirit! It may mean moving across the street. It may mean moving across the States. It may mean moving across the seas. How flexible are you? It may not involve a move at all, only a willingness.

Chuck Swindoll

GREATNESS

LETTER NUMBER

I'm sure it comes as no surprise to most of us that we act out precisely what we take in. In other words, we become what we think.

Long before that familiar line found its way into Psychology 101 and hyped-up sales meetings, the Bible included it in one of its ancient scrolls.

It just said it in a little different way: "For as he thinks within himself, so he is" (Prov. 23:7).

The secret of living a life of excellence is merely a matter of thinking thoughts of excellence. Really, it's a matter of programming our minds with the kind of information that will set us free. Free to be all God meant us to be. Free to soar! It will take awhile, and it may be painful—but what a metamorphosis!

Let me get to the heart of the issue. Since the mind holds the secrets of soaring, the enemy of our souls has made the human mind the bull's-eye of his target. His most insidious and strategic moves are made upon the mind. By affecting the way we think, he is able to keep our lives on a mediocre level.

Don't forget: Our minds were originally enemy-held territories. We were blinded by the power of the enemy. The mind was his "base of operations" until the light shone within. At that time, the veil was lifted and we were no longer blinded. It was a supernatural event in which new life was given, and the enemy was relieved of his command.

But I am increasingly more convinced that Satan doesn't want to give up his territory. He is a defeated foe who knows his future. Yet he fights to the last degree to maintain the hold he has had on us.

God is interested in our breaking free from such locks.

And what is God's ultimate goal?— To take "every thought captive." When He invades those lofty areas, His plan is to transform the old thoughts that defeat us into new thoughts that encourage us. He has to repattern our whole way of thinking. And He is engaged in doing that continually because old habits are so hard to break.

God's offer is nothing short of phenomenal! Remember it? It is "taking every thought captive to the obedience of Christ."

DREAMS

LETTER NUMBER

There is an important dimension to hanging tough that you dare not miss. It is the thing that keeps you going. I call it a dream.

I don't mean those things we experience at night while we're asleep. No, by dream, I mean a God-given idea, plan, agenda, or goal that leads to God-honoring results.

Most of us don't dream enough. If someone were to ask you, "What are your dreams for this year? What are your hopes, your agenda? What are you trusting God for?" could you give a specific answer? I don't have in mind just occupational objectives or goals, although there's nothing wrong with those. But what about the kind of dreaming that results in character building, the kind that cultivates God's righteousness and God's rulership in your life?

Here are a few more ideas about dreams. Dreams are specific, not general. Dreams are personal, not public. God doesn't give anyone else my dreams on the online computer screen. He gives them to me personally. They're intimate images and ideas. Dreams can easily appear to others as extreme and illogical. If you share your dreams with the crowd, they'll probably laugh at you because you can't make logical sense out of them. Dreams are often accompanied by a strong desire to fulfill them. And they are always outside the realm of the expected.

Sometimes they're downright shocking.
They cause people to suck in their breath,
to stand staring at you with their mouth open.
A common response when you share a dream is,
"You've gotta be kidding! Are you serious?"

One more thought on dreams: This is
the stuff of which leaders are made. If you don't
dream, your leadership is seriously limited. To
make things even more complicated, those who
refuse to dream the impossible are always in the
majority. Those who choose to live by sight will
always outnumber those who live by faith.

So once you've decided to live differently,
let God be your guide and hang tough—follow
your dreams with determination.

Chuck Swindoll

People
who soar are
those who refuse
to sit back and wish
things would change.

PURPOSE

LETTER NUMBER

Monotony and mediocrity mesh like teeth in gears. One spawns the other, leaving us yawning, bored, and adrift.
In referring to monotony, I do not have in mind a lack of activity as much as a lack of purpose.

We can be busy yet bored, involved yet indifferent. Life becomes tediously repetitious, dull, humdrum, pedestrian. In a word, blah.

Look into the faces of entertainers off the stage. Talk to physicians out of the office and hospital corridors. Those in the political arena are equally susceptible. Show me an individual who once soared, whose life was characterized by enthusiasm and excellence, but who no longer reaches those heights, and I'll show you a person who has probably become a victim of the blahs.

A blah attack may sound harmless, but it can leave us in an emotional heap, seriously questioning if life is worth it.

Yet even during your drab and seemingly meaningless assignments of life, God is there! He cares! He knows! From your yesterday to your tomorrow—God. From the little involvements to the big ones—God. From the beginning of school to the end of school—God. From the assignments that will never really make the headlines (which seems to be mere busy work) all the way to those things that gain international attention— God. He is there!

So the very next time you feel those clammy, cold fingers of the blahs reaching around you, remember, "From yesterday until tomorrow, You, O Lord, are there. You care!"

Chuck Swindoll

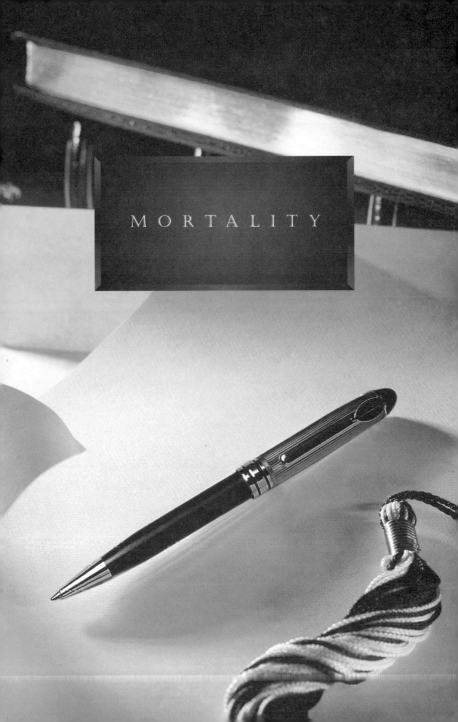

MORTALITY

LETTER NUMBER

*Life is so short.
We really don't have
many years. And to spend
them doing dumb stuff
seems like such a waste.*

I was intrigued several years ago when reading about some ghost towns littered across the plains of Nevada. The writer pointed out that there was every indication between the middle and the end of the 1800s that these towns would flourish forever. There were people by the thousands. There was gold in abundance. There were new buildings, vast plans, a spirit of excitement. There was wild and woolly entertainment at every corner—houses and hotels, brothels and taverns, mines and money. The Gold Rush looked as if it would last forever. But suddenly; everything screeched to a halt. Almost overnight those bustling, loud population centers became vacant dust collectors. The sound of the cash register ceased.

Today, except for a handful of eccentric desert dwellers, the stores and streets are empty. Those windswept ghost towns are now silent, hollow shells along forgotten sandy roads. Whatever happened to the boomtowns of Nevada?

What often looks as if it is here to stay and make a perpetual impact can be frighteningly temporary. When God says, "That's it; that's curtains," it's only a matter of time. It is the perspective in all of this that holds us together. Our God is in complete control. He lets nothing out of His grip. He starts one and stops another. He pushes one ahead and holds another back.

Yet our Lord is not some tyrannical God who stomps across heaven like the giant in Jack in the Beanstalk, swinging a club and waiting to give us a smashing blow to the head. No. Rather, it is as if He says to us, "You're Mine and I want you to walk in step with Me. I've arranged a plan so that walking with Me will result in a righteous lifestyle. If you make a decision not to walk with Me, I've also arranged consequences that will happen and you must live with them."

Yes, life is short. Yes, our sins are obvious; no one can deny that. But instead of thinking of these days as just about as futile as emptying wastebaskets, see the significance of them in light of God's plan. Ask him to help you view each day as He looks at it. He has a way of balancing out the good with the bad.

Chuck Swindoll

Never quit
because someone
disagrees with you.

DETERMINATION

LETTER NUMBER 12

When Jesus tells us to "seek first the kingdom of God," the very word "seek" implies a strong-minded pursuit. J. B. Phillips paraphrases the idea with "set your heart on." The Amplified Bible says, "Aim at and strive after."

The Greek text of Matthew's Gospel states a continual command: "Keep on continually seeking. . . ." The thought is determination, which I define as "deciding to hang tough, regardless."

We need to keep in mind the difference between natural sight and supernatural vision. When we look at life with vision, we perceive events and circumstances with God's thoughts. And because His thoughts are higher and more profound than mere horizontal thinking, they have a way of softening the blows of calamity and giving us hope through tragedy and loss. It also enables us to handle times of prosperity and popularity with wisdom.

I'll be frank with you. I know of no more valuable technique in the pursuit of successful living than sheer, dogged determination. Nothing works in ministry better than persistence— persistence in godliness, determination to stay diligent in study, persistence in commitment to the priorities of ministry, determination in working with people. I often remind myself of those familiar words in 2 Timothy 4:1, "Preach the word; be ready in season and out of season." That's a nice way of saying, "Hang tough! Do it when it comes naturally and when it is hard to come by. Do it when you're up, do it when you're down. Do it when you feel like it, do it when you don't feel like it. Do it when it's hot, do it when it's cold. Keep on doing it. Don't give up."

That is persistence and determination. Staying at it. Hanging tough with dogged discipline. When you get whipped or when you win, the secret is staying at it.

Chuck Swindoll

LAUGHTER

LETTER NUMBER

I know, I know—"life is serious business." If I hear that one more time, I think I'll gag. I fully realize that too much humor can become offensive. I recognize that it can be taken to such an extreme that it is inappropriate.

But doesn't it seem we have a long way to go before we are guilty of that problem? The final result of a joyless existence is sad—a superhigh-level intensity, borderline neurotic anxiety, an absence of just plain fun in one's work, a lack of relaxation, and the tendency to take ourselves much too seriously. We need to lighten up! Yes, spirituality and fun do go well together.

Scripture speaks directly to this issue, you know—especially the Proverbs:

A joyful heart makes a cheerful face, but when the heart is sad the spirit is broken (Prov. 15:13).

Amazing how that proverb goes right to the heart of the problem (no pun intended). We're not talking about a person's face here as much as we are about the heart. Internal joy goes public. We can't hide it. The face takes its cue from an inside signal.

A well-developed sense of humor reveals a well-balanced personality. Maladjusted people show a far greater tendency to miss the point in a funny remark. They take jokes personally. They take things that are meant to be enjoyable much too seriously. The ability to get a laugh out of everyday situations is a safety valve. It rids us of tensions and worries that could otherwise damage our health.

You think I'm exaggerating the benefits? If so, maybe you've forgotten another proverb: "A joyful heart is good medicine, but a broken spirit dries up the bones" (Prov. 17:22). Isn't that eloquent? Literally, it says, "A joyful heart causes healing." What is it that brings healing to the emotions, healing to the soul? A joyful heart. And when the heart is right, a joyful countenance accompanies it!

Chuck Swindoll

LETTER NUMBER

Reflect on God's gifts to you. In case you need a little help, read through Psalm 103.

Bless the Lord, O my soul; and all that is within me, bless His holy name. Bless the Lord, O my soul, and forget none of His benefits; who pardons all your iniquities; who heals all your diseases; who redeems your life from the pit; who crowns you with lovingkindness and compassion; who satisfies your years with good things, so that your youth is renewed like the eagle. The Lord performs righteous deeds, and judgments for all who are oppressed (Ps. 103:1–6).

The psalmist lists several benefits to prod our thinking. As we reflect on God's gifts to us, it's helpful to be specific.

Do you have eyesight? It's a gift. Do you have a good mind? It's a gift. Do you have leadership abilities that cause others to follow? A good education? These are all gifts. Has He given you a family? Has He given you sufficient clothes? How about a nice, warm, soft bed at night or a comfortable place to live in the hot summer? Why, some even have more than one home! These are all gifts from God's hand. Reflect on His numerous gifts to you. It will increase your joy. And a smile will soon replace that frown.

Remind yourself of God's promises regarding generosity. God promises if you sow bountifully, you will reap bountifully. So give! Give abundantly! Even extravagant giving is honored by God. I've never known anyone who went bad because he or she was too generous. Remind yourself of His promises regarding generosity and start giving!

Don't be afraid of outgiving God. It is absolutely impossible to do that. He will keep every one of His promises related to generosity. Try Him!

Chuck Swindoll

Never use age
as an excuse.

INDIVIDUALITY

LETTER NUMBER

One of the great American myths is that we are all a bunch of rugged individualists. We would like to think that, but it simply is not true. There are some exceptions, of course, but for the majority it is not that way at all.

Deep within, we imagine ourselves as a mixture of Patrick Henry, Davy Crockett, John Wayne, and the prophet Daniel! But the truth of the matter is that most of us would do anything to keep from being different. We'd much rather blend into the woodwork. One of our greatest fears is being ostracized, rejected by "the group." Ridicule is a pain too great for most to bear.

There are other fears—fear of being made to look foolish, fear of standing out in a crowd, fear of being talked about and misunderstood. Rather than rugged individualists, we are more like Gulliver of old, tied down and immobilized by tiny strands of fear, real or imagined. The result is both predictable and tragic: loss of courage.

Over thirty years ago I worked as a machinist in a shop where the vast majority were members of the local union. It didn't take me long to realize that the maintenance of a mediocre standard was one of the unwritten laws of that shop. Pressure was applied to anyone who worked unusually hard or produced more than the lower-than-average quota. Why? It made all the others look bad, and there was no way they would tolerate such a thing! Mild suggestions, if unheeded, would be followed by gentle nudges. Then, if still unheeded, the nudges would be followed by direct confrontation. If that was ignored, there were stronger measures taken to maintain the level of mediocrity. They would have no part of excellence. Conform or else!

Such pressure is not uncommon in numerous slices of life. The hard–charging high achiever at school is usually viewed with suspicion, not respect. Instead of others in the class picking up the pace and trying their best to do better, they would rather put down the student out front and make him or her look foolish. People don't want anyone to soar, especially if they prefer to slump!

Chances are good that you feel the same pressure I'm illustrating. If not, color yourself fortunate. Few are the places today where eagle types pursuing excellence are admired and encouraged to reach greater heights.

GODLINESS

LETTER NUMBER

I need to be very candid with you. If you are a "Sunday Christian," you will not stand alone when outnumbered. Apart from a personal and vital faith in Jesus Christ, it is impossible to wage a winning effort against the system called "the world."

Trying to overcome the powerful magnet of the majority without help from above would be a frustrating and counterproductive effort. Only God can give us such transforming power through our faith in His Son.

As far as God is concerned, a consistent godly life is well-pleasing, acceptable to Him. As far as you are concerned, it is an act of worship. It is a "spiritual service of worship."

We are like tiny islands of truth surrounded by a sea of paganism, but we launch our ship every day. We can't live or do business in this world without rubbing shoulders with those driven by the world's desires. God calls very few to be monks in a monastery. So we must make a practical decision not to be conformed while we are in the system, and at the same time, we must make a radical decision to give God the green light to transform our minds.

At the deepest level, even though the majority may not want to admit it, most people are conformists. That is why it is correctly termed a radical decision. Only a radically different mindset can equip folks like us to stand alone when we're outnumbered.

It takes courage to think alone, to resist alone, to stand alone—especially when the crowd seems so safe, so right. But remember God. Keep flying high like an eagle—far above the glue that snares the crowd. Up there it doesn't just seem safe and right, it is safe and right.

Chuck Swindoll

LEADERSHIP

LETTER NUMBER 17

If we hope to demonstrate the level of excellence modeled by Jesus Christ, then we'll have to come to terms with the kingdom we are going to serve: the eternal kingdom our Lord represented and told us to seek (Matt. 6:23) or the temporal kingdom of today.

Let's pause long enough to understand what I'm referring to when I mention the *kingdom*. It's one of those terms we like to use but seldom define.

Generally speaking, *God's kingdom is a synonym for God's rule.* Those who choose to live in His kingdom (though still very much alive on Planet Earth) choose to live under His authority.

For centuries God has been at work reestablishing His rulership. Jesus' words in Matthew describe the problem:

"No one can serve two masters; for either he will hate the one and love the other, or he will hold to one and despise the other. You cannot serve God and mammon. . . .

"For all these things the Gentiles eagerly seek; for your heavenly Father knows that you need all these things. But seek first His kingdom and His righteousness; and all these things shall be added to you" (6:24, 32–33).

All this leads me to some helpful news, some bad news, and some good news! The kingdom is the invisible realm where God rules as supreme authority. That's *helpful news.* The *bad news* is that we, by nature, don't want

Him to rule over us; we much prefer to please ourselves. We don't want anybody other than ourselves ruling over us! Much like those people in a story Jesus once told, "We do not want this man to reign over us!" (Luke 19:14).

Now, the *good news*. We don't have to live that way. God has given us an avenue of escape. It's called a birth from above. And not until we experience a spiritual rebirth will we submit to God's rule.

So when I write of God's kingdom, I'm referring to His rightful authority over our lives. I remind you—only by letting Him reign in your life can you experience true excellence.

Chuck Swindoll

God has a way
of balancing out the
good with the bad.

HOPE

LETTER NUMBER

Can you remember a recent "gray slush" day? Of course you can. So can I. The laws of fairness and justice were displaced by a couple of Murphy's Laws.

Your dream dissolved into a nightmare. High hopes took a hike. Good intentions got lost in a comedy of errors, only this time nobody was laughing. You didn't soar, you slumped. Instead of "pressing on the upward way," you felt like telling Bunyan to move over as you slid down into his Slough of Despond near Doubting Castle, whose owner was Giant Despair. Discouragement is just plain *awful*.

One of the greatest benefits to be gleaned from the Bible is perspective. When we get discouraged, we temporarily lose our perspective. Little things become mammoth. A slight irritation, such as a pebble in a shoe, seems huge. Motivation is drained away and, worst of all, hope departs.

God's Word is tailor-made for gray-slush days. It sends a beam of light through the fog. It signals safety when we fear we'll never make it through. Such big-picture perspective gives us a hope transplant, and within a brief period of time, we have escaped the bleak and boring and we're back at soaring.

God has an ultimate goal in mind: that we might have hope. And what leads to such a goal? Two things: perseverance and encouragement from the Scriptures. Again, the goal is hope. God has not designed a life of despondency for us. He wants His people to have hope. And He says such hope comes from the teaching of the Old Testament. Through endurance and through encouragement from the Scriptures, we can gain hope.

He promises us hope—relief from discouragement. Yes, it's available. And we can actually stand firm through discouraging times but only if we apply His instructions. Hard as it may be for you to believe, you will be able to walk right through those "gray slush" days with confidence. The One who gives perseverance and encouragement will escort you through the down days, never leaving you in the lurch.

Discouragement may be awful, but it is not terminal.

Chuck Swindoll

PERSPECTIVE

LETTER NUMBER

Almost every week I come into contact with people who have been misled, thinking that success depends solely upon talent or brilliance or education.

But the list doesn't end there. For some it's getting the breaks, pulling the right strings, having the right personality, being in the right place at the right time, knowing the right people, playing their cards right.

You see, it is our natural tendency to focus on the external, to be overly impressed with that which is seen. Wouldn't it be wonderful to develop the ability to look at a heart? Wouldn't it be great to be free of the limitations of strictly physical sight so that we could read hidden character traits?

Frankly, I think those who are physically blind often see more than those of us who are sighted. They often perceive much more than we can in the tone of a voice or in the sound of approaching footsteps or in the grip of a handshake. But we who have sight usually lack this insightful depth perception; the ability to detect the deeper things, the unspoken, the character, the hidden condition of the unspoken. And although God is able (and willing) to give us this ability, it isn't something we're born with.

I'd like to make three significant observations.

First: Age has little to do with achievement and nothing to do with commitment.

Second: A godly walk is basic to a positive life.

Third: Convictions are a matter of choice, not force.

We must keep on continually pursuing— seeking to see life from the heart.

Chuck Swindoll

Never think your choices obligate anyone else.

GUIDANCE

LETTER NUMBER

God offers instruction, but then it's our move. We must accept His instruction and apply it to our lives. Then, and only then, can we expect to cash in on the benefits of His instruction. So you see, application is the essential link between instruction and change.

Imagine, if you will, that you work for a company whose president found it necessary to travel out of the country and spend an extended period of time abroad. So he says to you and the other trusted employees, "Look, I'm going to leave. And while I'm gone, I want you to pay close attention to the business. You manage things while I'm away. I will write you regularly. When I do, I will instruct you in what you should do from now until I return from this trip." Everyone agrees. He leaves and stays gone for a couple of years. During that time he writes often, communicating his desires and concerns. Finally he returns. He walks up to the front door of the company and immediately discovers everything is in a mess—weeds flourishing in the flower beds, windows broken across the front of the building, the gal at the front desk dozing, loud music roaring from several offices, two or three people engaged in horseplay in the back room. Instead of making a profit, the business has suffered a great loss. Without hesitation he calls everyone together and with a frown asks, "What happened? Didn't you get my letters?" You say, "Oh, yeah, sure. We got all your letters. We've even bound them in a book. And some of us have memorized them. In fact, we have 'letter study' every Sunday. You know, those were really great letters." I think the president would then ask, "But what did you do about my instructions?" And, no doubt, the employees would respond, "Do? Well, nothing. But we read every one!"

In the very same way, God has sent us His instruction. He has preserved every word of it in a Book, the Bible. It's all there, just as He communicated it to us. When He returns for His own, He is not going to ask us how much we memorized or how often we met for study. No, He will want to know, "What did you do about my instructions?"

ACCOUNTABILITY

LETTER NUMBER

What do we mean by accountability? In the simplest terms, it is answering the hard questions. Accountability includes opening one's life to a few carefully selected, trusted, loyal confidants who speak the truth—

who have the right to examine, to question, to appraise, and to give counsel.

People who are accountable usually have four qualities:

Vulnerability—capable of being wounded, shown to be wrong, even admitting it before being confronted.

Teachability—a willingness to learn, being quick to hear and respond to reproof, being open to counsel.

Availability—accessible, touchable, able to be interrupted.

Honesty—committed to the truth regardless of how much it hurts, a willingness to admit the truth no matter how difficult or humiliating the admission may be. Hating all that is phony or false.

That's a tough list! As I look back over those four qualities, I am more than ever aware of why accountability is resisted by the majority. Those with fragile egos can't handle it. And prima donna types won't tolerate it. They have a greater desire to look good and make a stunning impression than anything else. I mean, "the very idea of someone probing into my life!"

Don't misunderstand. I'm not suggesting for a moment that accountability gives the general public carte blanche access to any and all areas of one's private life. If you will glance back a few lines you will notice I referred to "a few carefully selected, trusted, loyal confidants." They are the ones who have earned the right to come alongside and, when it seems appropriate and necessary, ask the hard questions, to serve in an advisory capacity, bringing perspective and wisdom where such may be lacking.

In our society, where privacy is a reward of promotion and a life of virtual secrecy is the prerogative of most leaders, a lack of accountability is considered the norm. This is true despite the fact that unaccountability is both unwise and unbiblical, not to mention downright perilous!

Today we need others to hold us accountable. Sometimes an objective opinion will reveal a blind spot. Sometimes we may simply need a sounding board to help keep us on target. Just remember—not one of us is an island. We need one another.

Chuck Swindoll

COURAGE

LETTER NUMBER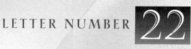

Someone once wrote, "Sow a thought, reap an act. Sow an act, reap a habit. Sow a habit, reap your character. Sow your character, reap your destiny."

Standing tall when tested takes courage—constant, relentless, never-give-up courage! You can be sure that the old flesh will fight for its arousal and satisfaction. All it takes is a little rationalization—just a little. Just look the other way. Just shrug it off. Don't sweat it. And before long you have a rattlesnake in your sleeping bag.

First: *Standing tall starts with the way we think.* It has to do with the *mind.* As I've said so often, being a person of inner strength is really a mental factor. It has to do with the way we think about God, ourselves, and others. Then it grows into the way we think about business, the way we think about dating, the way we think about marriage and the family, the way we think about the system that is designed to destroy faith and bring us down to a lower standard.

Second: *Standing tall calls for strong discipline.* This has to do with the *will.* Disciplining the eyes, the ears, the hands, the feet. Keeping moral tabs on ourselves, refusing to let down the standards. People of strength know how to turn right thinking into action—even when insistent feelings don't agree.

Third: *Standing tall limits your choice of personal friends.* This has to do with *relationships.* What appears harmless can prove to be dangerous. Perhaps this is as important as the other two factors combined. Cultivate wrong friendships and you're a goner. This is why we are warned not to be deceived regarding the danger of wrong associations. Without realizing it, we could be playing with fire.

Sow the wind and, for sure, you'll reap the whirlwind. Eagles may be strong birds, but when the wind velocity gets fierce enough, it takes an enormous amount of strength to survive. Only the ultrapowerful can make it through the whirlwind.

Chuck Swindoll

It takes courage
to think alone,
to resist alone,
to stand alone—
especially when
the crowd seems
so safe, so
right.

PRINCIPLES

LETTER NUMBER

I think we need to sign a mental declaration of independence. Let's put our name on the line, pledging ourselves with firm resolve, much like those brave men did on July 4, 1776, in Philadelphia when they signed the Declaration of Independence.

Did you know that of the fifty-six courageous men who signed that original document in Philadelphia, many did not survive the war that followed? Five were captured by the British and tortured before they died. Nine others died in the Revolutionary War, either from its hardships or its bullets. Twelve had their homes sacked, looted, burned, or occupied by the enemy. Two lost their sons in battle. One had two sons captured. Yes, the price of freedom was high indeed for those men. But deciding to be free, to think and live independently, to soar above the masses is always a costly decision.

In today's vernacular, committed individuals live with shallow tent pegs. They may own things, but nothing owns them. They have come to terms with merchandise that has a price tag and opted for commitment to values that are priceless.

Denying oneself is not to be equated with losing one's uniqueness or becoming of no value. There have been great people in each generation who modeled self-denial as they made significant contributions to humankind.

For years I taught that we are to "count the cost." It seemed so plausible. But suddenly one day, it dawned on me that Jesus never once told His followers to count the cost. No—He's the One who has already done that. He is the King who has already determined what it will take to encounter and triumph over life's enemies. And what will it take? A few strong, quality-minded champions whose commitment is solid as stone. And the cost will be great.

Chuck Swindoll

LETTER NUMBER

Picture for a moment the barrenness and bleakness that happens in a life when compromise occurs. It doesn't come immediately. At first it's fun to run with the wrong crowd.

There's some zip, a little excitement; there's a measure of thrill and pizzazz in being a part of the in-group. But inevitably the fleshly investment starts to yield its carnal dividends. And when that happens you suffer as you've never suffered before.

Perhaps the words "very low" paint a picture of bleakness that describes you at this very moment. You have ignored God's warnings and pushed your strong convictions aside as you associated with the wrong crowd. But now you are at the end of your rope. You're discouraged. You have failed miserably. You're thinking, What a terrible way to live!

All of us have spent time in that miserable camp called Reaping What Was Sown. En route, there's enough pleasure to make it seem like fun, but when it's all said and done, it's downright awful. There is no discouragement like the discouragement that comes from self-generated wrongdoing. Enduring the consequences of one's own irresponsibility creates feelings of grief and discouragement that defy description.

That's enough about the problem. What we really need are specific suggestions that get us back on track.

First, you need to openly acknowledge what caused your condition. Openly admit that you have failed to stand alone as a true child of God. You see, you weren't built to live that way. You have allowed someone else to call your cadence. You're marching out of step with your Instructor. And the Lord speaks directly: "You have not obeyed Me."

Second, focus directly on the Lord, not on the odds against you. Everything depends on where your focus is. You must discipline yourself to focus directly on the Lord, not on those odds!

Get this straight and never forget it: You will not stand alone when outnumbered or stand tall when tested or stand firm when discouraged if your focus remains on the odds. Your eyes must be trained on the Lord.

Chuck Swindoll

TEMPTATION

LETTER NUMBER

*May I remind you
of four of the more
powerful perils that can
level even the mightiest?
They are fortune, fame,
power, and pleasure. Each
works overtime to win a
hearing, to gain a foothold,
to woo us in.*

Whether subliminal, subtle, strong, or supreme, these messages search for chinks in our armor as they appeal to our natural appetites. "Get rich!" (fortune). "Become known!" (fame). "Gain control!" (power). "Be satisfied!" (pleasure). Each of these attractive snares invites our attention, holds out a juicy carrot, makes beautiful promises; yet each is an enemy always crouching and ready to plunge. Being masters of deceit, these messages employ one favorite method throughout our lives—*temptation*.

Let me mention a very practical thing about temptation. I have found that if I can stop the process fairly early, I'm safe. But if I leave my hiding place and venture toward the bait, there is a point of no return. I cannot turn around. If I go that far, I'm sunk.

So how can we have victory over temptation? First, *our natural focus must be counteracted*. Openly confess your weakness. Hide nothing. Use Scripture memory to replace sensual thoughts with spiritual thoughts.

Second, *our leisure time must be guarded*. Cultivate a plan, perhaps an exercise program, an intensive reading program, a hobby, a series of practical projects to occupy your time. Watch out for those video movies! If necessary, keep the television off. And stay away from the magazine rack.

Third, *our close companions must be screened*. Take a good look at your circle of friends. Do an honest evaluation of those with whom you spend personal time. I can offer you a principle you can bank on: Until you clean up your companionships, you'll never clean up your life.

Fourth, *our vow to God must be upheld*. Just as jealously as we would guard the marriage vows, we're to guard our promises to God and our commitment to purity.

Excellence—moral, ethical, personal excellence—is worth whatever it costs. Pay the price. Start today! Nothing less will ever satisfy you or glorify God.

Even in a world
where the
majority says,
"We can't,"
you can.

FRIENDSHIPS

LETTER NUMBER

The world in which
one person lives is too
limited and restricted.
When rubbing shoulders
with another, we gain a
panoramic view, which
allows us to see the
whole picture.

"As in water face reflects face, so the heart of man reflects man" (Prov. 27: 19). That's so picturesque! People provide a clear reflection of what is in the heart. A mirror goes only skin deep. The counsel of a friend reflects what is down inside.

I'm talking about people who love you too much to let you play in dangerous traffic. They also love you too much to let you start believing in your own stuff. When they spot conceit rearing its head, they say so. But they also love you too much to let you be too hard on yourself. Like Jonathan with David, they are messengers of great encouragement.

"He who walks with wise men will be wise, but the companion of fools will suffer harm" (Prov. 13:20). That statement is not a verse written to teenagers in high school, though it certainly would apply. I clearly remember my high school years, don't you? Many of us ran around with others who were tougher than we, so we could cover up our own feelings of inadequacy. My mother kept saying to me, "Charles, every time you run with the wrong crowd, you do wrong. When you are with the right crowd, you do right." Her counsel is still

true. If I were to run with the wrong crowd,
I would be tempted to do wrong.

And it doesn't stop when we turn twenty.
It goes on into adult years as well. If you choose
a wrong set of co-workers, you'll practice
wrong things in your business. If you choose
a wrong set of friends, you'll practice wrong
things in your social life. Run with those who
do drugs, and you'll wind up doing the same.

But—the flip side—those who walk with
the wise learn from them. You need someone
who will say, "I'm not sure how healthy that
is. I'm glad you asked me. Let's talk about it."
And that person will help point out the traps
you could fall into if you kept tracking in
that direction.

Other eyes, more perceptive and objective
than ours, can see traps that we may fail to detect.

Chuck Swindoll

DISTINCTION

LETTER NUMBER

The essential question isn't difficult to state: How can I, a person who has absorbed so many years of mediocre thinking, change? How can I, like a caterpillar, move from squirming in the dirt to enjoying the sweet nectar in God's creation?

As in the caterpillar's case, a radical metamorphosis must occur. It is a process that will be difficult, demanding, and lengthy—but, oh, how sweet the results! If you are really serious about conquering mediocrity (which, remember, starts in the mind), then I have three words to offer—memorize, personalize, and analyze.

Memorize. In order for old defeating thoughts to be invaded, conquered, and replaced by new, victorious ones, a process of reconstruction must transpire. The best place I know to begin this process of mental cleansing is with the all-important discipline of memorizing Scripture. I realize it doesn't sound very sophisticated or intellectual, but God's Book is full of powerful ammunition! And dislodging negative and demoralizing thoughts requires aggressive action. I sometimes refer to it as a mental assault.

Personalize. Here's where the excitement intensifies. As you begin the process of replacing old, negative thoughts with new and encouraging ones, put yourself into the pages of the Bible. Use I, me, my, mine as you come across meaningful statements.

Analyze. Instead of continuing to tell yourself you are little more than a helpless victim, take charge! As soon as you catch yourself responding negatively or defensively, think—analyze the situation. Then ask yourself a few tough questions. "Why am I getting so hot and bothered by this?" Or "Is there something I'm afraid of?" Or, maybe, "Am I reacting negatively because I have a reason or simply because I've formed some bad habits?"

Maybe the challenge to memorize, personalize, and analyze seems too simplistic to you. Perhaps you expected something else. You really expected some high-powered "secret" to success. No, I have no quick 'n' easy secret, no overnight-success pill you can take. Perhaps the best single-word picture is *visualize*. Mentally visualize being on a higher plane. Then once you "see it," begin to believe it and behave like it!

CONTENTMENT

LETTER NUMBER

Let's take a brief look at greed. Practically speaking, greed is an inordinate desire for more, an excessive, unsatisfied hunger to possess. Like an untamed beast, greed grasps, claws, reaches, clutches, and clings—stubbornly refusing to surrender.

The word *enough* is not in this beast's vocabulary. Akin to envy and jealousy, greed is nevertheless distinct. Envy wants to have what someone else possesses. Jealousy wants to possess what it already has. But greed is different. Greed is forever discontented and therefore insatiably craving, longing, wanting, striving for more, more, more.

The Greeks had a curious word they used when referring to greed. The word means "a thirst for having more." To illustrate, it's probably fanciful yet fairly descriptive to think of a fellow who is thirsty taking a drink of salt water, which only makes him thirstier. His thirst causes him to drink even more, which ultimately results in making him terribly sick. And if he continues to drink he could die.

That's the whole point of greed. You'll want more and more of something that really isn't good for you. And in the getting of it, you'll suffer the painful consequences. That is why Jesus warns, "Beware. Be on your guard. This thing is like a cancer—an insatiable leech that will suck the life right out of you." Enough will never be enough. Life does not—cannot—revolve around things if one hopes to achieve true excellence.

There's nothing in the world wrong with making a nice living. Nor is there anything wrong with being eminently wealthy if you earn and handle it correctly. But there's something drastically wrong when you keep it all to yourself! God gave it to you so you could, in turn, give it back to Him, to others—yes, in abundance. The only reason I can imagine for God's allowing anyone to make more than one needs is to be able to give more. We certainly can't take it with us, that's for sure!

Chuck Swindoll

God
deserves our
very best; nothing
more, nothing less,
nothing else.

LIFESTYLE

LETTER NUMBER

We live in a negative, hostile world. Face it, my friend, the system that surrounds us focuses on the negatives: what is wrong, not what is right; what is missing, not what is present; what is ugly, not what is beautiful;

what is destructive, not what is constructive; what cannot be done, not what can be done; what hurts, not what helps; what we lack, not what we have. You question that? Pick up your local newspaper and read it through. See if the majority of the news doesn't concern itself (and the reader) with the negatives. It's contagious!

This negative mindset leads to incredible feelings of anxiety. Surround most people with enough negatives and I can guarantee the result: fear, resentment, and anger. Negative information plus hostile thinking equals anxiety.

We are also engulfed in mediocrity and cynicism (a direct result of living in a negative world). Without the motivation of divinely empowered insight and enthusiasm, people tend toward the "average," doing just enough to get by. Thus, the fallout from the system is mediocrity. The majority dictates the rules, and excitement is replaced with a shrug of the shoulders. Excellence is not only lost in the shuffle, whenever it rears its head, it is considered a threat.

That's why most people choose not to live differently. Those who take their cues from the system blend into the drab backdrop of the majority. Words like "Just go with the flow" and

"Don't make waves" and "Who cares?" begin to gain a hearing.

Stop and think. In a world where all that cynicism is present, what is absent? Courage! That strong muscle of character that gives a nation its pride and gives a person the will to excel is gone.

I challenge you to be different, to stand apart from the crowd, with inner fortitude and strength of character—be disciplined to remain consistent, strong, and diligent regardless of the odds or the demands. Have courage!

Chuck Swindoll

EXCELLENCE

LETTER NUMBER

Mediocrity is fast becoming the by-word of our times. Every imaginable excuse is now used to make it acceptable, hopefully preferred. Budget cuts, time deadlines, majority opinion, and hard-nosed practicality are outshouting and outrunning excellence.

Those forces seem to be winning the race.
Incompetence and status quo averages are held
up as all we can now expect, and the tragedy
is that more and more people have virtually
agreed. Why worry over the small stuff?
Why bother with the genuine now that the
artificial looks so real? If the public buys it,
why sweat it?

To make it painfully plain, why think
clearly since most folks want someone else to
think for them? Why live differently in a society
where it's so much easier to look the same and
swim downstream? Why fight fiercely when so
few seem to care? Why stand courageously if it
means risking ridicule, misunderstanding, or
being considered a dreamer by some and a fool
by others?

Why, indeed? To quote young David just
before he took on that Philistine behemoth in the
Valley of Elah, "Is there not a cause?" Must we
wait for someone else to establish our standard
or to set our pace? Not on your life! It is my
firm conviction that those who impact and
reshape the world are the ones committed to
living above the level of mediocrity. There are
still too many opportunities for excellence, too

much demand for distinctiveness, to be satisfied with just getting by.

Excellence is a difficult concept to communicate because it can easily be misread as neurotic perfectionism or snooty sophistication. But it is neither. On the contrary, it is the stuff of which greatness is made. It is the difference between just getting by and soaring—that which sets apart the significant from the superficial, the lasting from the temporary.

A commitment to excellence is neither popular nor easy. But it is essential. Excellence in integrity and morality as well as ethics and scholarship. Excellence in physical fitness and spiritual fervor just as much as excellence in relationships and craftsmanship.

Since it is the living Lord in the final analysis who appraises our excellence, it is He whom we must please and serve, honor and adore.

Chuck Swindoll

P.S.

It lies before you now...
  the untrod path,
    the unopened door,
      the mountain peak,
        the broad, blue heavens.

I challenge you. Walk that path, open
that door, climb the mountain heights. The sky's
the limit.

Let God be your guide and hang tough—
follow your dreams with determination.

And when you find yourself inundated
with choices, don't be afraid. Be wise.
Choose God's way—choose excellence.

My prayers are with you.

WHOOPI GOLDBERG

Sugar plum Ballerinas

Plum Fantastic

WHOOPI GOLDBERG

Sugar Plum Ballerinas

Plum Fantastic

with Deborah Underwood
Illustrated by Maryn Roos

JUMP AT THE SUN BOOKS
New York

First Edition
1 3 5 7 9 10 8 6 4 2
Printed in the United States of America

This book is set in 13 pt. Baskerville BT.
Designed by Roberta Pressel

Reinforced binding

Library of Congress Cataloging-in-Publication Data on file
ISBN 978-1-4231-1173-3 (hardcover)
ISBN 978-0-7868-5260-4 (paperback)

visit www.jumpatthesun.com

Chapter 1

I look at myself in my bedroom mirror—the mirror with little pink ballet shoes painted around it, which is on top of the dresser with the little pink ballet shoe drawer handles, which is beside the lamp with the little pink ballet shoes on the shade, which is next to my bed, which has—you guessed it—little pink ballet shoes on the comforter and pillowcases.

You might think the person who just moved into this room likes ballet. You would be wrong. My mom is the ballet-crazy one. Ever since I was born, she's had her mind set on one thing: turning me into a ballerina. She even stuck me with Petrakova for my middle name. Alexandrea *Petrakova* Johnson! The closest I've ever been to Russia is Atlanta. At least until we moved here to Harlem last week.

After I packed all my ballet stuff up, I told one of the Muscle Men Movers it would be okay if they lost that particular box. I even

wrote *lose this box* on the side in purple felt pen in case they forgot.

But when Aunt Jackie dropped us off at our apartment on 123rd Street, there it was, right on top of the mountain of moving boxes in our living room. So out came the ballet mirror and

the ballet lamp and the ballet comforter and the ballet pillowcases. They looked bad enough in my old room, but at least I'd gotten used to them there. My new room is a wall-to-wall ballet nightmare. The good thing is that we're way up above the street. Maybe if I put my fan just right, the ballet stuff will blow out the window.

Just as I think that, I look at the ballerina posters on the wall (all courtesy of Mama, naturally). There's Maria Tallchief, who danced with the New York City Ballet. Virginia Johnson, who was the prima ballerina of the Dance Theater of Harlem. Janet Collins, the first black prima ballerina of the Metropolitan Opera Ballet. They stare down from their frames with stern looks on their faces, their eyes fixed on me as if they can tell I'm thinking Bad Ballet Thoughts.

The only person on my wall who's smiling is my idol, champion speed skater Phoebe

Fitz. Aunt Jackie gave me an autographed poster of her for my last birthday. Phoebe looks as out of place among all the ballerinas as I feel in my ballet-themed room. I imagine Phoebe giving me an encouraging wink; then I turn back to the mirror.

A skinny nine-year-old looks back at me. I have Mama's brown skin and my dad's mixed-up eyes—one is green and one is brown—and my hair is dark and wavy, just long enough to stick in a ponytail.

Phoebe Fitz is really strong. She does one hundred push-ups every day. I can only do twenty-three so far, but I'm pretty sure I can see arm muscles popping out already.

I look good, except for one major problem: I'm wearing a big old pink puff pastry, the tutu to end all tutus. Layers and layers of netting droop down to my knees. Little rhinestones sewn into the netting glint like diamonds in pink marshmallow cream. A row of pink roses marches around my waist, and silver ribbons flutter when I move.

Ugh. I'll bet Phoebe Fitz never had to wear a tutu.

"Mama, you *know* we aren't supposed to wear this junk to class!" I yell down the hall. No response.

I march into her workroom, the tutu flopping up and down like it's trying to take off. There are moving boxes everywhere, but instead of unpacking, Mama's gluing huge feathers onto what was once probably a nice hat. She mostly makes costumes, but she's been on a hat kick lately. I know Mama is very talented—lots of people have said so—but to *me*, that hat looks like an ostrich's backside. Loose sequins in a rainbow of colors shimmer on the floor.

Mama doesn't notice me come in. Normal people hang out in jeans at home, but not her. She's wearing one of her creations; she calls it the Gold Mine Dress. She got the idea for it from a book about the California gold rush. The skirt of the dress is supposed to look like a mountain, so it flares out at the bottom. When Mama's standing still, the only colors you see are chocolate brown and gray, like soil and rocks, but when she moves you can see flashes of gold from the shiny threads and beads she's sewn deep into the creases. She loves it, but says it doesn't read well onstage. That means it looks good close up, but from far away you'd miss the interesting details. ("Interesting details" are things that make clothes special. I wish my tutu did not have so many of them.)

The hat she's working on would read well onstage even if the stage were on Mars and you were looking at it from Earth. "Fabulous . . . *mm-mmm*, perfect; maybe one more orange . . ." she says to herself as she chooses feathers and holds them up to the hat to see how they look.

The ballet school letter is lying by her sewing machine. I wave it in front of her face. "Mama!"

She looks up, a little dazed. I'd be dazed too if I'd been staring at purple and orange feathers all morning. "Why, Alexandrea!" she says, standing up to look me over. "You look wonderful. All ready for class?"

"Mama, listen to this." I read from the letter. *"Students at the Nutcracker School shall wear standard ballet leotards and tights. Dress code shall be strictly enforced."*

Mama puts down the feathers. "You *are* wearing a leotard. It's fabulous and *unique*. Can you imagine how it will stand out onstage?" She strikes a dramatic pose, as if an audience of 3,000 were watching her every move.

Sure, the tutu would look great onstage. However, I am not going onstage. I am going to a ballet class at a strange school in a strange city. Mama seems to have missed this critical point.

"And it doesn't say you can't wear a tutu over the leotard," Mama continues. "You *are* wearing those gorgeous tights I set out for you, yes?" She tries to peek at my behind, but I hold the tutu down. The tights I'm wearing are one of Mama's favorite creations. The legs look like normal tights, but the rear end is covered with shiny pink lightning bolts. You have to wear them over your leotard, not under, or you wouldn't be able to see the lightning (which would be fine with me). Mama calls the outfit Girl Power—Girl for the tutu and Power for the lightning. She says the contrast between the delicate tutu and the powerful lightning makes an interesting artistic statement. The dress code says we're supposed to wear tights, not interesting artistic statements. At least no one will see them under the tutu.

"Mama, *pleeeeease*." Thinking about the new ballet class makes my stomach hurt. I won't know anyone. I won't know where the bathroom is. And on top of all that, I get to walk in looking like an electrified bride on a wedding cake.

Mama drops the feathers and puts her hands on her hips. "Alexandrea, that is enough. When I was growing up, I dreamed of taking ballet from Ms. Debbé at the Nutcracker School, but my mother couldn't afford it. Now that my own little girl is going, she is going in style. Understand?"

It's hopeless. "Yes, ma'am."

"You only have one chance to make a first impression, you know," she says. "When they see you in that creation of mine, I guarantee you'll stick in their minds that way forever."

That's what I'm afraid of.

Chapter 2

Ten minutes later, we're walking down Madison Avenue. It's early June, and I'm hot and sticky in the jacket I threw on to hide my outfit. Horns honk and music blasts from cars and windows. Little kids run through sprinklers in the park across the street. Mama's happily pointing out places she knew when she was a kid. "That's where your Aunt Jackie and I played after school. . . . That's where my friend Roberta lived. . . ."

I'm not really listening. I'm thinking about Georgia. The street where we lived

11

was quiet, with big trees and lots of grass. My best friend, Keisha, lived down the street. Best of all, the Apple Creek ice rink was just two blocks away. Last summer, Keisha and I went almost every afternoon.

One day Mama came to the rink to walk me home. "I've got a surprise," she said as we walked through the grass oval in the middle of Leland Park. "You and your mama are moving to Harlem." She had a big old grin on her face, like this was the best news in the world.

I stopped walking. I felt all shivery and clammy and prickly, like someone had tossed a bucket of Coke on me.

"Why?" I asked. But in my heart, I already knew. The bridal shop Mama owned always had a lot of customers. Mama showed them her fabulous designs: the Japanese-inspired kimono gown with fabric cherry blossoms trailing behind; the purple straight-up-and-down dress with the matching straight-up-and-down hat that looks like an oatmeal box; the fire-and-water dress that has flames of orange and red beads licking its hemline and a river blue shawl. But the brides all wanted normal white wedding dresses with normal white veils.

Mama sat on the ground. She took my hand and pulled me down beside her. The cool grass tickled the backs of my legs. "Honey, if I have to make one more boring wedding dress, I'll go crazy. I've always dreamed of having my own costume business, and you know it won't happen here in this little town. I want to do better—better for myself, and better for you."

I didn't need her to do any better for me. We had a nice house. We had a van. I had ice skates. I didn't need anything else. I started to tell her, but she kept talking.

"And I miss New York. I only moved here because of your daddy, and you know how long it's been since he passed."

My dad died when I was just two. It

sounds weird, but I don't really miss him, because I can't even remember him.

Mama said there was lots of potential in New York, because of all the theaters on Broadway. She said it would be great to live close to Aunt Jackie, who owns a hair salon and could braid my hair in all sorts of fancy ways.

I folded my arms across my chest. "Are there ice rinks there?" I asked.

"Yes, including a very famous one," she said. "And so many cultural opportunities. You'll love it. A change will be good for both of us." She stood and pulled me up. "Now what would you say to a triple scoop of Chocolate Coma ice cream? I think I hear it calling your name."

Before I knew it, Mama sold our van, because, she said, no one drives in New York. (If no one drives here, who's in all these cars?) And three weeks later we'd moved into a stuffy apartment on the third floor of a building called a brownstone. There's not even an elevator—just a creaky stairway that sounds as if it should be in a haunted house. (I run up the stairs really fast in case there are any ghosts around.)

So now I'm walking down a noisy Harlem street with a river of sweat pouring down my back. One thing about New York: Mama fits in a lot better here. Some people stare at the Gold Mine Dress. But they stare in an admiring way, not in the what-on-earth-is-she-wearing-now? way they did in Apple Creek.

Still, I'd rather be home. If I were, I'd be heading out right about now to skate with Keisha. "Where's the famous ice rink?" I ask.

"It's down at Rockefeller Center," Mama says. "We can go there when it gets cold." A fire engine zooms by, lights flashing and siren screeching. I plug my ears till it passes.

"Mama, how am I going to win an Olympic speed skating medal if I don't skate till it gets cold? Everyone knows you gotta practice all the time."

"Baby, speed skaters wear boring old bodysuits—"

"Skin suits," I interrupt.

"Boring old skin suits, then. They are aesthetically unappealing. All those speed skaters look exactly the same. They look like the little guys in that old chocolate factory movie."

"Oompa-loompas?" I say. "Oompa-loompas are short and orange. Can you name one short orange speed skater?"

She goes on as if I hadn't said anything. "Ballerinas get to wear beautiful costumes."

"But, Mama . . ."

An old man pushing a shopping cart nearly runs over my foot. Mama yanks me out of the way.

"You need to pay attention, Alexandrea," she

says. "We aren't in Apple Creek anymore. Here in Harlem you need to use your city smarts." Just as she says this, a girl about my age races by on a skateboard, knocking into Mama's bag.

"Sorry!" the girl yells out as she passes. She screeches to a stop in front of a building, and her baseball cap flies off. She scoops it up, flips her board into the air, catches it, and races up the steps.

As the door slams behind her, I look at the glass sparkling over the doorway. THE NUT-CRACKER SCHOOL OF BALLET, the gold letters read. In smaller letters below, it says, WE TURN LITTLE GIRLS INTO LITTLE LADIES.

Mama hmmphs. "If the sign is right, they've got some work to do with *that* little girl," she says.

I glare at the sign above the door as Mama pulls me up the stairs. She can make me take ballet. She can make me wear a twinkling tutu. But *no one* is turning me into a little lady.

Chapter 3

Mama pushes open the door, and we go inside. The Nutcracker School is the weirdest-looking ballet school I've ever seen. Well, okay, I guess I've never actually seen a real ballet school before. My ballet class in Apple Creek was held in a church-Sunday-school building. All the classrooms were in a neat row off the main hallway. We met in the biggest room, where they had the church potlucks. The bathroom was at the end of the hall, with a big sign telling you where it was so you didn't have to ask anyone.

The Nutcracker School looks like a super-size house. There's a little office right at the front, and a room off to the left where girls are sitting and waiting for their class. Some of them look up as we pass. They're all dressed like the kids in my Apple Creek ballet class were: in normal ballet clothes. I was hoping that all the parents in New York ignored dress codes. Nope.

A sign saying CLASS IN SESSION hangs from a wooden door on the right. I wonder if there's just one classroom till I see the staircase leading up to the next floor. The sounds of piano music and thuds—maybe people practicing their jetés (that means "jumps," in ballet talk)—are coming from upstairs. Every time there's a thud, the chandelier above the stairs rattles, and the ceiling creaks as if it's going to break.

Also, I do not see any bathrooms. Maybe people in New York just hold it.

A tall, handsome man with caramel-colored skin and a short beard comes down the stairs, sees us, and smiles. He's wearing a bright white T-shirt and stretchy black pants, and he smells like pine trees.

He sticks out his hand. "I'm Mr. Lester. You must be Mrs. Johnson."

Mama takes his hand. "*Ms.* Johnson. I'm not married." She gives him a big, toothy smile. I roll my eyes.

"And you must be Alexandrea." He turns to me. "I'm one of the teachers here."

I try not to look surprised. We didn't have men ballet teachers in Apple Creek.

"Would you like to take off your coat?" he asks.

I shake my head. Mama gives me a look. I slowly peel off my jacket, hoping it's smashed some of the puff out of my tutu. But the skirt pops right back out, like one of those monsters in a scary movie that you think is dead until it jumps up and kills some-one. Some of the girls in the waiting room stop talking to gape at me.

Mr. Lester's eyes fly open. "What an . . . uh, interesting outfit," he says.

"I made it myself." Mama beams. "It's one of a kind."

"It certainly is," Mr. Lester murmurs. "But Alexandrea might be more comfortable wear-ing a plain leotard next time."

Mama ignores this. "Alexandrea has been *so* looking forward to meeting Ms. Debbé," she says, which is a total lie. "It's her dream to be a prima ballerina with the Harlem Ballet, just like Ms. Debbé was." This is a total lie, too! I've never even heard of the Harlem Ballet. Next time she tells me not to fib, we are definitely having a discussion.

"I'm afraid Ms. Debbé is away at a dance teachers' conference," Mr. Lester says. "I'll be teaching Alexandrea's class today."

"Lucky Alexandrea," Mama says, winking at him.

I've had about all I can take of this. "Mama has to go now," I say in a loud, clear voice. "She has some very important costumes to make." I nudge her toward the door.

"Make me proud, sugar," Mama calls. She waves at Mr. Lester from the steps.

"Now, Alexandrea," Mr. Lester says. "Most of the nine-year-olds are in the Ballet Three class. We'll try you out there and see how you do. Any problems, you come talk to me. Okay?"

I nod. I wonder if I can keep up with kids who have been going to a big-city ballet school.

Mr. Lester takes me on a tour. We clomp up the stairs to the second floor, where there are studios. There's a big room on the third floor where they do their shows. There's a little room where they store costumes and music, and Ms. Debbé has an office down a hallway.

And there are bathrooms. Whew.

He takes me back downstairs to the room where the girls are waiting for class. "I'll leave you here," he says. "Class will start in ten minutes." He smiles at me. "I know it's not easy being the new kid, but I think you'll have a good time. It's a nice bunch of girls."

"Yes, sir," I say. I take a deep breath and go in.

Chapter 4

The waiting room gets quiet when I walk in. A few girls sitting near the door snicker. I hang my jacket on one of the hooks lining the wall, head to the bench farthest from the snickering girls, and start to sit down. Then I remember the lightning bolts on my behind. They make a weird crinkling sound when you sit on them. I stay standing.

I see the girl with the skateboard. I blink. She's sitting with two other girls. All three of them have skin so black it almost looks blue, and high cheekbones, like models are supposed to have. Their faces are almost identical. But the skateboard girl has muscles like she's on the Phoebe Fitz Push-Up Program, and the girl in the middle looks like she eats the skateboard girl's dessert for her. The one on the end is skinny but not muscley. She has her hair tied back with pink ribbons. The rounder one is holding a notebook and gazing off into space.

The wall in front of me has framed posters from the Harlem Ballet that Mama just mentioned—I guess it really does exist. I pick out one poster and focus on it. Maybe if I stand still, like a statue, everyone will forget I'm there.

But one girl marches right up to me. Her

honey-colored hair falls in spi-
ral curls around her shoulders, and she's wearing a
bright red-and-orange leo-
tard with green tights. Her
outfit stands out almost as much as mine does,
but she doesn't look one bit embarrassed.

"Girl, what *are* you wearing that crazy
thing for?" she asks in a loud voice.

I stare at her. In Georgia it's not nice to
point out weird stuff about people. A man
could walk down the street with a pig on his
head and everyone who saw him would just
smile and say how nice the weather was.

She gazes back at me with brown eyes, eyes
that look like they don't miss a thing. She
seems to be waiting for an answer.

"My mama made me," I explain.

"Wow. You got one *loca* mama," she says,
shaking her head.

"Loca?"

"I guess you don't know Spanish. *Loca* means 'crazy,'" the girl says. She starts warming up one foot at a time, drawing circles in the air with her toes.

My ears start to burn. Sure, *I* think Mama's a little crazy, but that doesn't mean some strange kid gets to say so.

"Did your mama pick *your* outfit?" I ask. "'Cause she might be *loca*, too."

Will this make the girl mad? I get my best don't-you-mess-with-me look ready, just in case. But instead she smiles and spins around like a fashion model. "You like it? I dyed the leotard myself. Actually, I dyed it because I spilled spaghetti sauce on it. My parents own an Italian restaurant, so lots of my clothes end up orange. I'm Epatha. Who are you?"

"Alexandrea," I say.

"You're from the South, right? My second-grade teacher was from Atlanta, and he talked like you."

All these people sound funny to me—I'd forgotten I must sound funny to them, too. I nod. "I just moved here."

"*Benvenuta*. That means 'welcome' in Italian," she says.

She sounds like she really means it. I smile.

"Are you Italian or Spanish?" I ask.

"I'm part Italian, part Puerto Rican, and all fabulous," she says, doing another twirl. I laugh, and she grins back at me.

"So you can speak Italian *and* Spanish?"

She shrugs. "My Puerto Rican grandma and my Italian grandma both live with us." She takes a purple ponytail holder off her wrist and twists her hair back into a bun. "I'm the only one in our family who speaks everything. My dad says I should come with subtitles."

I look over at the skateboard girl and the others again. "Are those girls triplets?"

"Yup," says Epatha. "JoAnn has the skateboard. Jerzey Mae is on the end, with the pink ribbons. Jessica writes poetry. One of her legs is shorter than the other, so she wears special shoes."

I'm trying to remember all this. I'm thinking so hard I almost forget how I'm dressed.

Two girls in pink leotards walk in. They both have their hair pulled back into buns. One of them is wearing a sparkly tiara. "I didn't know it was Halloween," Tiara Girl says to her friend as they walk past me. They dissolve in nasty giggles.

"Don't worry about them," Epatha says. "They think they're all that, and they ain't."

I'm impressed, both by her attitude and by the fact that she says "ain't." If I said "ain't," Mama would ground me for a week.

"Look at the way they walk," she continues. "Their feet stickin' out like duck feet. They saw a ballerina walk like that in a movie, I bet." She looks at them. "Quack," she says loudly. "Quack, quack."

Mr. Lester walks in and claps. "Time for class, ladies."

By now there are almost two dozen of us in the room. We follow Mr. Lester up the stairs to a studio on the second floor. A long barre runs along the window side of the room. The other wall is covered with mirrors. An old lady with bright red hair and green glasses is playing wild jazz on a piano.

"Class is starting now, Mrs. Buford," Mr. Lester tells her.

She sighs as if he's cramping her style. She stops playing.

Mr. Lester tells us all to sit on the floor. Epatha gives me a funny look. I hope she can't hear the lightning crinkle. I sit very still.

Mr. Lester welcomes us to the Nutcracker School's Ballet Three class. He tells us Ms. Debbé will teach the class most of the time, and that the class meets two times a week: Tuesdays and Saturdays.

"I'm pleased to announce that we have two new students with us. When I call your name, please stand up. . . ."

He looks at me. I shake my head wildly. In this getup, the last thing I need is more attention. He stops for a minute, then says, ". . . Or just raise your hand, so we know who you are."

I decide Mr. Lester is okay.

"Candace," Mr. Lester calls out. A mousy-looking kid pops up and down fast like a jack-in-the-box.

"Welcome, Candace. Alexandrea?" he says.

I raise my hand.

"Alexandrea just moved here from Georgia," he says. "We hope you'll enjoy our class."

"Yes, sir," I say.

"*Sir?*" says Tiara Girl. A few other girls laugh.

"In the South, children are taught to respect adults. Not a bad idea," Mr. Lester says. Tiara Girl snorts.

He continues. "I know you'll all be excited to hear about the show we'll be doing at the end of this session."

Epatha pokes me and whispers, "The best kid gets to be the Sugar Plum Fairy and do a dance all by herself."

Whoa. I thought the Sugar Plum Fairy was a Christmas thing. I wonder if New York is like Australia, where the seasons are all mixed up and Christmas comes when it's hot out.

"I'm gonna be the Sugar Plum Fairy this year," Epatha says. She turns to a short girl behind us. "Right, Terrel?" Her eyes glint, as if she knows she's asking for trouble.

The girl is padded with what looks like baby fat, but she's still small; she's definitely younger than any of the other girls here.

Terrel exhales heavily, as if they've been over this a million times before. "You are *not*. I am," she whispers. She's got long braids tied up in a bun, and the crookedest teeth I've ever seen. When she eats a sandwich, the bite marks must look like they were made with those zigzag scissors Mama uses for sewing. I run my tongue behind my own teeth and feel how smooth and even they are.

Mr. Lester continues. "But I'll let Ms. Debbé tell you more about that when she returns next week. Now, ladies—barre, please. First position."

Everyone stands up and takes a place at the barre. We put our feet in first position, which is when your heels are together and your toes stick out. The piano lady starts playing tinkly ballet music.

"Demi-plié . . . grand plié . . . demi-plié . . . and up," Mr. Lester says as we bend our knees and go down to the floor, then back up, just like in my old ballet class. Epatha's in front of me, making arm gestures bigger than everyone else's. Every once in a while she adds in her own little jumps or arm swirls, but Mr. Lester doesn't seem to mind. When we turn around to do the other side, I'm behind Terrel. Her movements are tight and precise, as if she were in the ballet division of the U.S. Marines.

I can already tell this will be harder than my old class. My teacher in Apple Creek, Miss Gutchings, was about a hundred years old. She wore thick glasses that made her eyes look huge, but she still couldn't see us very well. She'd show us a move, then sit down in her chair and try to stay awake while we practiced it by ourselves.

Mr. Lester is definitely no Miss Gutchings. He's coming around and correcting each of us, moving an arm here, a leg there. Nothing gets by him. I haven't seen some of the barre exercises before, so I try to copy whoever's in front of me. Mr. Lester can always tell when I'm faking it. He comes by and quietly shows me the right way to do each new move.

After our barre work is done, Mr. Lester asks us to gather in the center of the room. We make a big circle.

"Let's do some turns," he says.

Uh-oh. Turns are not my strongest move. When you do turns, you're supposed to spot. That means you look in one place, then turn your head fast and look at the same place again. It keeps you from getting dizzy. But I just can't do it.

Keisha says I am spotting-impaired. When my class did turns in Apple Creek, I always crashed into the wall, unless I crashed into another girl first. Once I crashed into the watercooler and flooded the studio, which got even Miss Gutchings's attention. After that she made me sit on the side of the room during turns practice.

But that was a whole month ago. I've probably gotten better since then.

"We'll do simple chaîné turns." Mr. Lester

stands in front of us and does a series of turns, moving in a perfectly straight line along the mirrors. "We'll travel clockwise around the room."

The piano lady plays. Everyone starts doing neat turns. Everyone, that is, except me.

After just two turns, the room is whirling, and I can hardly stand up. I crash into the girl with the braids. "Sorry," I say.

I crash into Tiara Girl. "What is wrong with you?" she says.

I crash into the end of the barre. My tutu gets stuck on it. I hear a ripping sound, but luckily I don't see any holes when I inspect it.

Mr. Lester claps. "That's enough turning for today," he says loudly. I feel everybody's eyes on me. I look up at the ceiling.

"Let's practice our grand jetés," Mr. Lester says, eyeing me nervously.

Yes! That's one thing I'm good at. I love leaps. I saw a TV show about animals called gazelles that live in Africa. They look like deer, and they jump through the grass like nobody's business. When I do grand jetés, I feel just like a beautiful gazelle.

We form two lines, and two at a time we bound across the room. Epatha and I are second. We get a running start, then leap from one leg to the other.

"Very nice, Alexandrea," Mr. Lester calls as we walk back to the ends of our lines. Epatha bumps her shoulder against mine and grins. I beam.

A lady pops her head into the room. Mr. Lester goes over, and she says something to him.

"Keep going, girls," he says. "I'll be right back."

Epatha and I inch closer to the heads of our lines. Finally it's our turn again. I jump even higher this time, higher than Epatha. I soar through the air. I feel light, lighter than a balloon. The other girls gasp. I smile. I must be really good.

In midleap, I realize something is missing. My tutu. It's lying in a pile in the middle of the floor. And my pink-shiny-lightning-bolt-covered rear end is right out there, shimmering for everyone to see. I turn around to hide it, but it's too late. Everyone's laughing. Tiara Girl's laughing extra loud.

The piano lady stops playing. She leans over the piano to get a good look and moves her glasses up and down as if she can't believe what she's seeing.

I run over and grab the tutu. The girls circle around me, still laughing their heads off. It's just like on the gazelle TV show, when one of the leaping gazelles gets surrounded by a pack of nasty lions ready to rip her to bits.

Epatha pushes through, carrying a sweatshirt. "What are you all looking at?" She ties the sweatshirt around my waist and marches me out of the center of the circle. "Y'all better start jumping again before Mr. Lester gets back," she calls over her shoulder. "Mrs. Buford—how about some music?"

The piano lady's painted-on eyebrows creep up to the top of her forehead, but she begins to play. The other kids get back into their lines and start leaping.

"Thanks," I say to Epatha. I crumple up the stupid tutu and cram it under a chair.

"De nada," she replies. "Don't worry about it."

Mr. Lester comes back. He sees the sweatshirt around my waist but doesn't ask any questions. He's definitely okay.

After class, we all go downstairs to wait for our parents. I put on my coat fast and stuff the tutu into my bag. I'll tell Mama about the fashion disaster later.

Tiara Girl leaves with a tall woman in fancy clothes. "Bye, Electric Butt," she says with a smirk as she passes me.

I stick out my tongue at her back. Epatha grins.

Mama comes in and gives me a hug. "How'd it go, baby?"

I try to decide. "Okay, I guess."

"Did you make any new friends?" she asks as we walk down the steps.

Epatha and an older girl pass by us. "*A presto*—see you soon!" she calls to me as they turn down the street.

"Yeah," I say to Mama. "I think I did."

Chapter 5

The day after my first ballet class, I wake up when I hear Mama rattling around in her workroom. Not that it takes much to wake me up nowadays. It's hard to sleep in Harlem. The sounds of cars and music and talking drift up from the street to my bedroom window. I miss my room in Apple Creek. I miss the tree outside my window. I miss the squirrels that scampered around and tried to swipe each other's acorns.

"Morning, honey," Mama calls as I drag myself into the kitchen. She's wearing Queen of the Nile, a sand-colored pantsuit with a cascade of shimmering green and blue beads at the top. They narrow into a thin band that winds down the front and wraps around the left leg. The pantsuit is Africa, and the beads are the Nile River. I helped her find a map that showed exactly where the river twists and turns, so she'd know where to put the beads. The outfit is actually kind of cool, and she looks beautiful, as always. But sometimes I wish she'd just wear a robe at breakfast.

"What do you want?" she asks.

"Can I have oatmeal?"

"Oatmeal?" She stares at me like I'm nuts. "You've never had oatmeal in your life."

"I read in *Speed Skating Weekly* that Phoebe Fitz eats oatmeal for breakfast every single day," I say.

Mama rolls her eyes. "Even Phoebe Fitz wouldn't be crazy enough to stand over a hot stove cooking oatmeal when it's eighty-three degrees outside. Try again."

I sigh. "Okay. Cornflakes, I guess."

Mama goes to the cupboard and pulls out

a cereal box. It looks weird.

"Those aren't the right ones," I say. "There's supposed to be a scarecrow on the box."

"Honey, that's a Southern brand. They don't have it in New York. These are just as good." She pours milk over a bowl of cereal and sets it in front of me.

I shove my spoon into the bowl and stir the cereal around. "They're smaller. And lumpier. And they're a darker yellow."

"Alexandrea . . ."

"I'm eating them, I'm eating them," I say. If this place is so great, why can't they make normal cornflakes?

After I eat my unsatisfactory New York cereal, I help Mama unpack her workroom. She arranges bolts of fabric while I dump red, green, purple, silver, and gold sequins into little organizer drawers. I hang scissors from hooks on the wall. I put all the jumbled-up spools of thread in order, light yellow to dark yellow, light green to dark green, light blue to dark blue. We set hat stands around the room for all the fancy hats she's working on.

Pretty soon it looks just like her workroom back home. She steps back to admire our work. "A real, live, professional New York City costume studio," she said. "Now I can get to work advertising. With a little luck, those orders will start flying in."

They'd better. I heard her talking to Aunt Jackie last night. She said that moving here used up a lot of our money. No one's bought Mama's bridal shop back home yet. And even I know it costs more to live in a big city than in Apple Creek.

"I guess we'll have to move back if they don't," I say. I try to look disappointed at the prospect, but I can't keep the corners of my mouth from turning up. If we moved back, I could have the rest of the summer to skate with Keisha. And I could take ballet at a place where no one's crazy enough to make me do turns.

"Baby, this *is* our home now."

I try another tack. "If we can't afford my ballet classes, I understand."

She gives me a look. "Nice try. Now help me put these moving boxes away."

I sigh. Looks like I'm stuck—stuck in Harlem and stuck in ballet.

Chapter 6

Epatha is already at the Nutcracker School when I get there on Tuesday afternoon. She looks me up and down approvingly. "Much better."

I convinced Mama to let me dress like a normal person this time. I have on a light brown leotard and tights. Not only are they boring and non-attention-getting, but they may help me blend in with the floor if I keel over doing turns.

Epatha, however, would only blend in if she were in the middle of the Amazon rain forest. Her leotard and tights have all different kinds of green in them.

"No spaghetti sauce?" I ask.

She shakes her head. "I spilled pesto on these. You know what pesto is? It's green, 'cause it's made of ground-up *foglie*—leaves. You eat it on noodles."

Ground-up leaves? In Georgia people don't eat ground-up leaves. *Worms* eat ground-up leaves.

Two girls walk over to us. The taller one has dreadlocks and big brown eyes. The other one is Terrel, the short girl with crooked teeth who stood next to me in the last class. Today her braids are hanging down, and there's a butterfly barrette at the bottom of each one. She thrusts a stack of flash cards into Epatha's hand.

"*You* quiz Brenda," she says. "I can't even read some of these words. We don't learn about clavicorns in second grade."

"*Clavicles,*" says Brenda. She takes the top

flash card from the stack Epatha is holding and waves it under Terrel's nose.

"Why can't doctors just say 'collarbone,' like normal people?" Terrel asks as she pulls her braids back into a bun.

Brenda points to a word on the card. "Okay, *collarbone*."

"Whatever," says Terrel.

"Hey, Brenda. Where were you on Saturday?" Epatha asks.

Brenda seems to give up on getting any flash card help. She takes the cards back and sits on the floor, plopping her books down next to her. "Mom my with museum science the at show planetarium a to went I."

"Y'all, this is Alexandrea," Epatha says. "She's from the South, and sometimes her mama makes her wear crazy tutus. And this is Terrel," she says, pointing to the short girl. "She's only eight, but she's really good at ballet, so she's in our class. This is Brenda. She's going to be a doctor, so she studies all the time and talks backward."

I don't know if it's polite, but I have to ask. "Uh . . . why do you talk backward?"

"Backward wrote Vinci da Leonardo," Brenda says as she takes off her sneakers, which look old enough to disintegrate at any minute. "Smart really was he. Smarter get I'll, backward. . . ."

Terrel sighs loudly and holds up her hand to stop her. "Brenda, how's she supposed to understand you? She hasn't had a year to figure out backward talk like we have." She turns to me. "Some guy named Leonardo da Vinci wrote backward. He was real smart. So Brenda thinks if she talks backward, she'll get smarter. Like, it'll rewire her brain or something."

Brenda nods.

Terrel says, "Leonardo wrote each word backward, too, so *cat* turns into *tac*. Brenda tried talking like that, but even we couldn't understand her. So now she just puts the words in reverse order. It get?"

It get. I think for a second. *Get it.* I nod.

"We're the only ones who know what she's saying. It's useful when you're talking around grown-ups—it's like a code," Epatha adds.

"Me understand can't mom my even," Brenda says with a satisfied smile.

I'm trying to figure this out when Tiara Girl waltzes in with her friend. "How adorable," she says. "Gobbledygook Girl and Twisted Teeth are friends with Electric Butt." They sit down and put on their ballet slippers, leaving their sneakers under a bench.

Brenda ignores the girls—she's studying her flash cards again—but Terrel stares at them. When they disappear into the bathroom, she marches over and expertly ties Tiara Girl's shoelaces to the bench.

Just as Terrel returns, an older woman

glides into the waiting room. She's tall, and the green turban she's wearing makes her look even taller. Frosty green eye shadow pops out against her deep brown skin. She looks elegant and powerful all at the same time, like she's the queen of New York. She has a walking stick in one hand and a beautiful carved wooden box in the other.

She raises the stick into the air. Silence falls over the room.

"The class, it begins," she says. She turns sharply and heads upstairs, the filmy sleeves of her blouse trailing behind her. The stick thumps on each stair as she goes up.

"That's Ms. Debbé," Epatha tells me as we follow her up the stairs. "I bet she gives us the shoe talk."

"The what?" I ask.

"You'll see."

We sit on the studio floor. Ms. Debbé stands motionless in front of us. When the last girl sits down, Ms. Debbé sweeps her arm out to the side.

"Welcome to my ballet school," she says. Her accent sounds like that cartoon skunk's, so she must be French. "Here you will learn to move. You will learn to dance. But also, you will learn to live. Movement is dance. Movement is life. Dance is life." She looks around the room at us, as if she's daring us to say she's wrong.

What the heck is she talking about?

Epatha watches her raptly. Terrel looks at me and raises her eyebrows. Brenda's lost in space, probably thinking about clavicles.

Ms. Debbé opens the hinged lid of the carved wooden box. She takes out a pair of worn toe shoes and holds them in her hands so we can see them. "These shoes, these humble shoes"—she pauses dramatically—"are my most prized possession. They are the toe shoes of Miss Camilla Freeman." She shows us

the sole of the right shoe, which has a faded autograph written in black pen.

"Miss Camilla Freeman was my teacher when I first came to this country." She seems to stand even taller when she says this. "When Miss Camilla Freeman began dancing, people told her she would never be a star because of her color. But did she listen?"

She looks right at me and waits.

"Uh . . . no?" I say.

"No! She did not listen to those people, those foolish people. She worked hard. She became the first black prima ballerina in the Ballet Company of New York. Where she wore *these*." She waves the toe shoes in the air.

"These toe shoes," she continues, "represent potential. These toe shoes, they prove anything is possible."

"I'll bet those toe shoes prove shoes can still stink after fifty years," Epatha whispers to me. Ms. Debbé swivels her head to stare at

Epatha. Epatha shuts up fast.

"If you get discouraged, if you want to quit, if the amazing art that is the ballet seems too difficult for you, think. Think of these toe shoes." She tucks the shoes gently back into their box.

"Now. We talk about our show, our lovely show at the end of the summer."

You can tell most of the girls have heard the shoe talk before. Now they perk up and pay attention.

"This year, things, they will be different." Ms. Debbé raises an eyebrow and looks around the room, nodding her head.

Whispers fill the room. "Whoa. Things ain't never different around here," whispers Epatha. "The Ballet Three show is always the same. I know, 'cause both my sisters took this class."

"We will have some *thrilling* new dances," Ms. Debbé says.

Tiara Girl raises her hand. "Will we still have the Sugar Plum Fairy dance?"

"*Oui, oui,*" Ms. Debbé says. "But that, too, will be different. Before, always we chose the best dancer in the class to be the Sugar Plum Fairy."

"Well, duh," Epatha whispers. "Who else would they choose—the worst dancer?"

Ms. Debbé continues. "Last week, I was at a meeting of dance teachers. At the meeting, we discussed potential. You all have the potential to be great dancers. So, this year, how will we choose parts? By pulling your names out of a hat. You will all have an equal chance to be the Sugar Plum Fairy."

Whispers fill the room. The grin slides off Epatha's face. Terrel looks determined. Even Brenda's brow is creased. "Applications college my on good look would part the getting," she whispers.

Terrel exhales heavily. "You're only nine,

girl!" she says. "You got seven more years to worry about college applications."

Ms. Debbé raps her stick on the floor for attention. "We draw the names next class. Once they're chosen, no changes. No arguing. You must bloom where you are planted, children. *Bloooom,* like lovely little flowers! Now. To the barre."

After class, everyone is still talking about the drawing. The good dancers are upset because they were expecting to be the Sugar Plum Fairy. The not-so-good dancers are excited, because they have a chance now. Then there's me—all I want is to make it through class without breaking any bones.

We pack up our things. There's a shriek from the other side of the waiting room.

"Who tied my shoes to the bench?" Tiara Girl cries.

Terrel grins.

I skip outside to meet Mama. Ms. Debbé

may think we all have potential, but I *know* I don't. As far as ballet goes, I am a potential-free zone. I don't care who gets the Sugar Plum Fairy dance, as long as it's not me. The good thing is, it's not going to be. There are twenty-three girls in the class, and I never win anything. I don't even win when *everyone* wins. At Keisha's birthday party, they drew names out of a hat for prizes. Every person was supposed to get a prize, but my name fell out of the hat. They found it two days later in a pile of crumbs under the refrigerator.

I may have to take ballet, but one thing's for sure: I'm safe from the Curse of the Sugar Plum Fairy.

Chapter 7

"Come on, Alexandrea—get that lovely outfit on so we can go," Mama calls.

I look around my room. I do not see any lovely outfit. I do, however, see a blue-striped sailor suit with a pleated skirt and a straw hat. It looks like something a kid would have worn over a hundred years ago. That's because it *is* something a kid would have worn over a hundred years ago.

Today Mama says we are going to "implement the marketing plan." This means she's made appointments at a bunch of theaters to introduce herself and her work. Unfortunately, she wants to show them that she can do historical costumes as well as modern ones. And she wants to show them what her work looks like on a real person. Which means I get to dress like a kid who's escaped from an 1880s orphanage.

Mama pops her head into my room. She's wearing her Iceberg Suit. She got inspired to make it after we watched *Titanic*. It's white with shades of shimmery blue like a glacier. There's a pointy triangular cap over each shoulder, and there's a pointy triangular hat that goes with it. She says dressing like an iceberg is good on days like today, because an iceberg is a force of nature that can bring down even the strongest ship. I guess that means everyone will have to hire her.

"Come on, honey," she says. "Can't you figure out how it goes on?"

"I can't figure out *why* it goes on," I mutter. But I pull on the skirt and the top. Phoebe Fitz gives me a sympathetic look from the poster on the wall.

"Adorable!" Mama says, spinning me around.

"If you get a lot of business today, we never have to do this again, right?" I say.

"Right," she agrees.

Ten minutes later, we're tromping down the street. Ladies are pointing at me, and I can hear them telling each other how cute I look.

"Isn't this fun?" Mama asks, adjusting her enormous white sunglasses. We each have a load of fancy brochures for her costume business in our arms. It's so hot I can already feel the bottom one getting slippery and wrinkled from my sweat.

Mama's set up appointments all over town. When we get to a theater, she sashays in like she owns the place. She plunks a brochure down and tells whomever's listening exactly why they need to hire her. Everyone is polite, and they all promise to keep her information on file.

"Isn't anyone going to hire you *today*?" I ask.

"That's not the way it works, Alexandrea," she says. "You need to plant some seeds and hope some of them sprout."

I would not be a good businesswoman, because I don't like waiting for seeds to sprout. When I planted flower seeds back home, I kept digging them back up to see if they were doing anything.

After hours of this, we head back up Broadway toward home. I spot a big building with a fancy marquee out front. They probably have lots of money to hire costume people. "There's another theater," I say. "Aren't we going in that one?"

We stop right in front. "The Harlem Ballet," Mama says. "That's where Ms. Debbé danced when she was young. I always wanted to go see her, but back then we couldn't afford it."

Mama gazes up at the building as if it's

some kind of church or something. I've never seen her like this before. She looks like she's scared to go inside.

Suddenly I forgive her for making me wear a goofy outfit and dragging me around in the sweltering heat. I take her hand and pull her toward the entrance. "Well, now you're here. What are you waiting for?"

We push open the heavy door together and walk up to the box office. "Can I help you?" the ticket lady asks.

Mama just stands there. I poke her. She clears her throat, then launches into her spiel. She pushes a flyer through the window so the ticket lady can see it, and asks if she can make an appointment to talk with a costume person.

Footsteps echo on the floor behind us. I smell pine trees.

"Alexandrea?"

Oh, great—It's Mr. Lester. You'd think in a big city you wouldn't run into people you know. Wrong. This is as bad as back home, where if you weren't careful you'd see your teacher holding hands with her boyfriend at the ball game or buying athlete's foot cream at the store.

"Hi," I say. He gives me a funny look. I'd almost forgotten my sailor suit. The man is going to think I don't have any normal clothes at all. He, on the other hand, looks good, with his dark jeans and crisp yellow shirt.

Mama turns around and smiles real big. "Hello, handsome," she says. Looks like she's back to normal—too bad.

He asks what we're doing there, and Mama shows him a brochure. Then she asks what *he's* doing there, and he says he's directing one of the dances in the Harlem Ballet's next show.

Wow—that sounds like a pretty big deal. I wonder what a hotshot director is doing teaching ballet to a bunch of kids. And I wonder if

I'm going to be even more of a mess in his classes now, because I'll be all nervous.

"Would you like to see the theater?" he asks.

What I'd really like is to get out of there before Mama says anything else embarrassing. But I've never seen the inside of a New York theater before.

"We'd love to," Mama says.

He takes us through the hall with its red velvet seats, past the heavy curtain, and backstage. He shows us the dressing rooms (which are small and not all glamorous—there aren't even stars on the doors). We see the room in the very back of the theater where they control the lights, and the place where they store the costumes. Mama sneaks some brochures onto the costume designer's desk when Mr. Lester isn't looking.

We walk onto the stage and look out at the house, the place where the audience sits.

There must be hundreds of seats. Even though they're all empty, my stomach jumps a little.

"To think Ms. Debbé danced on this very stage," Mama says, turning around slowly.

"Oh, yes. Mom still feels like this is her home," Mr. Lester says. "That's why the Nutcracker School has such close ties to this theater. Many of our students go on to dance here."

Mama looks confused.

"Ms. Debbé's your mom?" I ask.

"Yes. She kept her maiden name, since she was already well known when she got married," he says.

Mama starts to get all flustered again. I guess if I met Phoebe Fitz's kid, I'd be freaked out, too. Mama looks a little sick, as if she went on a roller coaster too many times.

Mr. Lester thinks the heat must be getting to Mama. He takes us to a coffee shop across the street and buys us some cold drinks, which is nice of him. We sit in the window. Mama recovers enough to ask Mr. Lester if he has any ideas about where she should take her brochures, and he writes down the names of a few of his theater friends for her.

As they chat, I look up and see a face right outside the coffee shop window. I can't believe it—it's Terrel. I flush as I see her wide-open

eyes go from Mr. Lester to Mama and back again. Okay, this is totally *worse* than Apple Creek. I wave halfheartedly to her as a guy who must be her brother grabs her arm and pulls her away.

We say good-bye to Mr. Lester and begin to walk home. "That man is certainly handsome. When I first met him I wondered . . ." Her voice trails off, and then she shakes her head. "Well, now that I know he's Ms. Debbé's son I could never go out with him. Imagine having Ms. Debbé as a mother-in-law! I'd be too scared to even talk."

I'm relieved by this. But I wish Terrel were around to hear it.

Chapter 8

It's Saturday before ballet, and rain is pounding against the studio windows. I'm sitting with Epatha and Brenda. Terrel hasn't shown up yet. I don't want her to be sick, but I wouldn't mind if she went on vacation for a few months. But no sooner do I think this than she appears and comes straight over to us.

"What were you doing in that goofy sailor suit, and is your mom dating Mr. Lester?" she asks me.

"*Mr. Lester?*" say Epatha and Brenda at the same time. At least they ignore the sailor suit part.

"Of course not," I say. "We just ran into him when we went to the ballet theater. And he took us out for drinks."

"To a *bar*?" Epatha shrieks.

"Are you crazy?" I ask her. "To a coffee shop. It was no big deal."

Terrel squints. "It looked like a date to me," she says.

My face gets hot. "Well, it wasn't. He thought my mom was going to pass out from the heat, so he bought her a soda. That's it." I can hear how defensive I sound, which is stupid, since I'm not lying. "Did you know Ms. Debbé is his mom?" I add, hoping to distract them.

It seems to work. "That knew everyone thought I," says Brenda.

"That crazy lady," Epatha says. "Why would she want to pull the Sugar Plum Fairy's name out of a hat? It needs to be someone really good, *una persona muy buena*. Someone like me, for instance."

Terrel raises her eyebrows.

"Or you," Epatha adds, to be fair. "Or Brenda." She glances at the book Brenda's face is buried in. "Gross! What the heck is that?"

Brenda looks up from a colorful drawing that shows all the blood vessels in the human body.

"Dead be we'd, them without and, vessels blood it's. Gross not it's."

Terrel translates for me.

"Well, it's making me *enferma*," says Epatha.

"That's 'sick' in Spanish," Terrel explains. "She says it all the time."

With all the translating she's doing, Terrel could work for the United Nations.

Tiara Girl comes over. "Just so you know, I'm going to be the Sugar Plum Fairy, so don't hold your breath."

"How do you know?" Terrel demands.

Tiara Girl smiles. "My dad gives this school a lot of money. He called Ms. Debbé last night and told her he wants me to be the star. Too

72

bad *you* all don't have rich dads." She looks at us, especially at Brenda.

"Tiara that under around rattling brain a have don't you bad too," Brenda responds. As Tiara Girl is trying to figure out what she said, Mr. Lester comes in and claps.

"Class, girls," he says. He leads us upstairs, a long cardboard tube under his arm. He opens the studio door and we file inside.

Ms. Debbé drifts through the door carrying a top hat. It looks as old as Ms. Camilla Freeman's toe shoes.

"Ladies," she says. "It is our big day, the beginning of the exciting preparations for our performance. Your names, they are all in this hat. I will draw them. No funny business. No favorites." She gives Tiara Girl a tight smile.

Tiara Girl looks a little *enferma*.

Ms. Debbé continues. "First, we will have the Raindrop Ballet. The dancers will wear these lovely costumes." She nods at Mr.

Lester. He pulls a large paper out of the cardboard tube and unrolls it. It's a drawing of a blue leotard and blue skirt with little shiny raindrops hanging around the bottom. Most of the girls ooh and aah.

Brenda raises her hand. "Light refracts it way the of because blue looks just water."

Ms. Debbé looks at Terrel, who says, "She says raindrops aren't really blue."

Ms. Debbé replies, "Thank you, Brenda and Terrel. However, *our* raindrops *will* be blue. Now, then." She holds the hat. Mr. Lester pulls out six pieces of paper and reads six names. Six girls on the other side of the room high-five each other.

"Yes!" Epatha whispers when her name's not called. "I'm supposed to be a fabulous fairy, not a drippy raindrop."

"Next we have the Dance of the Animals," Ms. Debbé says. Mr. Lester holds up a paper showing ten different animal costumes.

Ms. Debbé reads off each animal, and then Mr. Lester pulls out a name.

Tiara Girl is a warthog. Epatha and Terrel laugh their heads off. Even Brenda smiles.

"Now, an exciting new dance I have just choreographed. It is called the Monster Ballet, and it will be very, very charming," Ms. Debbé says.

Mr. Lester unrolls the next paper. The costume looks like a big, hairy, purple grape. Everyone gasps. It is not a good gasp. This costume makes Tiara Girl's warthog outfit look like Cinderella's ball gown.

Brenda gazes at the picture with interest. "Bacteria coli E. like looks it," she says.

"What's E. coli bacteria?" asks Epatha.

"A germ that makes you throw up," Terrel says.

"*Sí*. Just looking at that picture makes me want to throw up," says Epatha.

"Our six little monsters will be . . . Brenda,

Terrel, Epatha, JoAnn, Jerzey Mae, and Jessica," Ms. Debbé says. Epatha sticks her tongue out the side of her mouth and collapses on the floor like she's been hit with an arrow.

I look around to see how the triplets are taking it. JoAnn looks bored. Jessica looks as if she's trying to make the best of it. Jerzey Mae looks like she's about to cry.

"Now, finally," Ms. Debbé says, "for our Sugar Plum Fairy."

Mr. Lester reaches into the hat.

Finally? I do some fast math in my head as she pulls the name from the hat. Six rain-drops, ten animals, six monsters, twenty-three kids in the class . . .

Oh, no.

"Alexandrea will be our Sugar Plum Fairy this year," Ms. Debbé says, beaming at me. Mr. Lester holds up a picture of a white dress with a white, sparkling tutu. Naturally. Another tutu.

"You will love the dance, Alexandrea," Ms. Debbé says. "It is very fun. Lots and lots of turns."

I feel sick.

After class, Epatha and the other girls are less friendly to me. "Lucky you," Epatha says.

"Lucky, yeah," says Brenda, as she jerks her T-shirt over her head.

Terrel looks as if she'd like to tie my legs to a bench.

What is wrong with these people? Is it my fault my name popped out of that hat? I'd rather have to wear an 1880s sailor suit for the rest of my life than be the Sugar Plum Fairy. "I really wish it wasn't me," I say, trying to sound calm, the way Mama does when she's mad.

"Oh, sure you do," says Epatha. "It's *such* a burden to be a star."

"Are you *sure* your mom isn't going out with Mr. Lester?" Terrel asks.

My scalp begins to prickle. Getting the part was bad enough, but now they think I'm a liar on top of it?

"My mom is *not* going out with Mr. Lester, and I do *not* want to be the Sugar Plum Fairy. I don't even want to be in the stupid show." So much for sounding calm. My voice gets higher and louder with every word.

Brenda looks skeptical. Epatha snorts.

"*Everyone* wants to be the Sugar Plum Fairy," Terrel says.

That does it. "*I* don't!" I yell. "How many times do I have to tell you? Doesn't anybody in New York have ears?"

Epatha's jaw drops open. I yank off my ballet slippers, put on my sneakers, and storm out the door.

Chapter 9

Mama's waiting on the steps under a bright blue umbrella.

"I hate ballet. I hate Harlem. Can we move back to Georgia?" I ask.

"What's the matter, baby?" she asks, putting her arm around my shoulders and pulling me under the umbrella.

"I have to be the stupid Sugar Plum Fairy in our dance show." I stomp through a puddle and immediately regret it as the water oozes through my sneakers into my socks.

Mama's face lights up. "The Sugar Plum Fairy? That sounds like a big part."

"It is," I growl. I'll be standing out, just like she wants. But I'll stand out for getting so dizzy I spin off the stage or for throwing up or something—probably not what Mama dreamed of.

"Well, that's wonderful, Alexandrea!"

"It is *not* wonderful. I can't do it. There are lots of turns, and I just about killed three people when we did turns practice."

"Now, sweetie. I'm sure they gave you the part because you're the best dancer. Ms. Debbé knows what she's doing."

"They drew my name out of a *hat*!" I yell.

"That is enough, Alexandrea Petrakova," Mama says.

"Fine," I mutter.

Mama stops walking and turns to face me. "Did you mean, 'yes, ma'am'?"

"No one says 'ma'am' around here," I tell

her. "I'm enough of a freak already. I dance like a freak. Do I have to talk like one, too?"

Being grounded is different in Harlem. In Georgia, it meant I couldn't go outside and play with my friends. Here I'm not supposed to go out by myself anyway, so Mama had to think of something different. So being grounded means I have to stay in my room. Luckily, I have a tiny TV in my room. Unluckily, being grounded also means Mama takes my TV away and puts it in her work-room. That way, she says, I'll have plenty of time to think about what I've done.

After an hour, I go into her workroom. She looks up from her sewing machine.

"I'm sorry I was disrespectful." I quickly add, "Ma'am."

"Thank you for your apology, Alexandrea." She hands me back my TV.

I sit on a stool beside her.

"Do I really have to take ballet? I want to be a speed skater, not a ballet dancer."

Mama looks at me. "Alexandrea, this is a whole new start for both of us. I want to make sure you don't miss any opportunities. We both have so much potential here in New York."

Potential again. If there does happen to be a tiny speck of potential in me somewhere, maybe I can have it surgically removed so everyone will leave me alone.

Mama sees me roll my eyes. She sighs. "I'll tell you what. You take the class till December. Really give it a chance, Alexandrea. It's important to me. If you still want to quit then, well . . ." She holds up her hands.

"Really?" I say. "I can?"

She nods.

"Thank you!" I put down the TV and jump into her arms.

"You have to give it your best shot, though. Deal?"

"Deal."

I skip down the hall to my room and plug in the TV. When I flip through the channels, I find a new show, *Swan Lake Smackdown*, where celebrities try to perform ballet dances.

This cheers me up. I may be bad, but these guys are terrible. A rock star clomps around like an elephant stuck in taffy. A famous football player flies into the air and falls over when he tries to do a chassé, which is kind of like a gallop. I laugh at them—until I think about the people who will be laughing at me when I try to do the Sugar Plum Fairy dance. Suddenly it's not so funny anymore.

I turn off the TV. Surely when the teachers see how bad I am, they'll give the part to some other kid. They wouldn't let me screw up the whole show.

Would they?

Chapter 10

When I walk into the waiting room before the next class, Epatha, Terrel, and Brenda are sitting together. Brenda says something—which, of course, I don't understand—and they all look at me. No one says hi. Okay, maybe I shouldn't have yelled at them. But *they* shouldn't have gotten all snippy about me being the Sugar Plum Fairy. I sit down on the bench farthest from them.

In class, we go through our barre exercises—*pliés, relevés, grand battements*. We move to the middle of the room to do floor work. I still struggle to keep up, but at least now I've seen all the moves before.

Halfway through class, Ms. Debbé says it's

time for us to start working on our dances. We split up into two groups. Ms. Debbé stays in the studio with the raindrops and the animals. Mr. Lester leads the monsters and me to one of the other classrooms.

The monsters are up first. Mr. Lester explains their dance to them. "You all know how little kids are scared of monsters in their closets, right?"

Jerzey Mae's eyes open wide. I'll bet she's *still* scared of monsters in her closet.

"For this dance, a Ballet One girl will be in a bed onstage. You'll come out of the closet and do a funny dance. She'll watch you, then chase you back into the closet. Got it?"

He shows them the first part of the dance, how they'll come in the door and gather around the bed to wake the little girl up. Then the girls line up and try it themselves.

Terrel and Epatha are really good dancers. Terrel does every move perfectly, like a windup doll. She gets all the steps right away. Epatha is good, too, but in a different way. She's wilder, with big jumps and big arm movements. She bugs her eyes out and makes scary faces. She really does look like a monster.

The triplets are the most interesting to watch. Jessica walks a little funny, but she dances well even with her special shoe. JoAnn, the skateboarder, picks up the steps almost as fast as Terrel.

But Jerzey Mae is a mess. She goes right when she's supposed to go left. She goes left when she's supposed to go right. JoAnn rolls her eyes and ignores her. Jessica tries to help, pointing her in the right direction when she messes up.

They go over the first part of the dance a few times. "Good work, girls," Mr. Lester says. He turns to me. "Your turn, Alexandrea."

My stomach clenches into a tight little ball. Fabulous—I get to make a fool of myself in front of a bunch of girls that hate me *and* a famous ballet director.

"You've heard of the ballet *The Nutcracker*?"

I nod. Mama makes me watch the DVD every Christmas. I always sit in front of her so I can take a little snooze without her knowing.

"There's a Sugar Plum Fairy in that who does a really flashy dance."

I must look as worried as I feel, because he laughs and adds, "Your dance isn't nearly that hard, I promise. But it uses the same music. Okay?"

Stalling seems like a good idea at this point. "Isn't that supposed to be a grown-up dance?"

Mr. Lester smiles. "Good point. When Ms. Debbé was a girl, she always wanted to dance the Sugar Plum Fairy, but the part always went to an adult. Now that she has her own school, a Ballet Three girl always gets to do a Sugar Plum Fairy dance."

"But why is it in summer?" I ask. I look at

the clock. If I can keep him talking for twelve more minutes, I'm home free.

"Lots of our girls dance in an adult dance company's *Nutcracker*, so it's hard for us to have a show during the holidays. So we put the Sugar Plum dance in our summer program." He raises an eyebrow. "Any other questions?"

He's on to me. I shake my head.

"So. You'll wear a beautiful, glittery, white dress—your mama will like that part— and do your dance to start off the Ballet Three program. Got it? Let's go."

I hope the other girls will leave, but they sit down on the floor to watch. Epatha folds her arms across her chest.

Mr. Lester shows me how I'll start off, frozen in the center of the stage with my arms spread out, a fairy wand in one hand. I can do that. I can't do turns, but I'm a genius at standing still.

Then I'm supposed to chassé to the left.

Then I chassé to the right. Mr. Lester shows me. I follow along behind him. So far, so good.

"Now you do four chaîné turns to the left," he says. He backs up and moves way across the room. Clearly he remembers how well I turn.

I turn once. I turn twice. I turn three times. I keel over.

Epatha whispers something to Brenda. My cheeks get hot. I pull myself up and try not to look at my ex-friends.

"Are you really spotting, Alexandrea?" Mr. Lester asks.

Well, I'm trying to. And there are definitely spots in front of my eyes. I nod yes.

"Hmmm," he says, rubbing his chin. "We'll need to work on that. Let's move on."

By the time class ends, we've gotten through the first part of my dance. Every time we reach a place where there are turns, I get dizzy and mess up.

"Hmmm," Mr. Lester says, rubbing his

beard again. "That's enough for today, girls. Go home and practice."

The other girls get up. Everyone ignores me except Jessica. She gives me a little smile, not in a nasty way but as if she feels bad for me. Maybe since her leg is messed up she knows what it's like not to be able to do things exactly right.

Each class after that, we spend a half hour all together doing our barre exercises and practicing moves. Then we split up to work on our dances. The monsters are always first. Their dance looks a little better every time they practice.

"Good work, Jerzey Mae," Mr. Lester calls out. Even she's getting better.

I am not getting better. I'm getting worse.

I still can't do turns. I can do the steps with Mr. Lester, but when I'm dancing alone I forget them. If I notice the other girls looking at me, I get nervous and make even more mistakes.

"Hmmm," Mr. Lester says over and over. He rubs his chin so much I'm surprised it's still on his face.

I try to practice at home. But how am I supposed to practice if I can't remember the steps?

I need to do turns in a straight line, so I try doing them in our hallway. I crash into one wall, then the other. When I knock a picture off the wall, Mama finally snaps at me: "What on earth are you doing, Alexandrea?"

"I gotta practice for my ballet show," I tell her.

She grumbles, but doesn't say anything else. She's been in a bad mood lately. Costume orders are not pouring in after all. There may be lots of theaters in New York, but it turns out there are lots of costume-makers here, too. I hear her whispering on the phone to Aunt Jackie at night. When I ask if we can fly home to Apple Creek for a visit, she says we can't be spending money on things we don't need right now. But then she tells me that worrying about money is her job, not mine. Which is good, because worrying about the recital is taking up all of my worry brain cells.

Saturday is especially bad. Mr. Lester tells me to go through my dance right from the start. I stand still at the beginning, the way I'm supposed to. Then I make the mistake of opening my eyes and seeing all the other girls reflected in the mirror, sitting in a row along the wall staring at me. My mind goes blank. I can't remember anything. I just stand there.

Mr. Lester turns the music off. "I would like to speak with Alexandrea alone," he tells the other girls. They file out of the room, sneaking looks back at me as they go.

"Alexandrea, I'm wondering if having you do the Sugar Plum Fairy dance is a good idea," Mr. Lester says. "Do you think you're going to be able to learn it?"

My eyes start to prickle. I blink hard. "I don't know," I say.

He looks at me kindly. "Why don't you think about it and tell me Tuesday. Talk to your mom about it. If you don't want to do it, we can find something else for you to do in the show. Maybe instead of having a Ballet One girl in the bed for the Monster Dance, it can be you."

I turn this over in my mind. Everyone in the whole school would know that I'd had to give up the Sugar Plum Fairy part because I was a terrible dancer. They'd all laugh at me. Mama would be so disappointed. She brought the Sugar Plum Fairy outfit home and sewed it up so it fit me perfectly. She even replaced some of the old lace and sequins.

But if I do the dance, I'll make an even bigger fool of myself. Would Mama rather have a daughter who was a coward, or one who embarrassed herself in front of an auditorium full of people?

"I'll think about it," I tell Mr. Lester. But I've already made up my mind. I just need to find a way to tell Mama.

Chapter 11

When I meet Mama after class, she's carrying three shopping bags full of fabric. She's in a great mood, because she finally found someone who needs some flashy dresses. It's a man who dresses up like a woman and sings show tunes in a theater. Mama's never made a dress for a man before, but she doesn't care. "Man, woman, crocodile, whatever—someone wants a dress and has the money, I'll make it," she says as we walk down 125th Street past the Apollo Theater. "Plus, this fellow understands what it means to make a theatrical statement."

We stop in and pick up a pizza to celebrate. She hums as she sprinkles red pepper flakes on her slice. I can't bring myself to tell her I'm a Sugar Plum reject. Maybe later.

After dinner she heads right to her workroom. She sings at the top of her lungs, and I can hear her sewing machine clattering away. I'll tell her tomorrow.

I turn on my little TV and channel surf. A basketball game, a dumb cartoon, and a game show . . . and there's *Swan Lake Smackdown* again.

I recognize a soap opera star leaping across the stage in tights. The lady he's dancing with looks nervous. I wonder how many times he's stomped on her toes. I'm about to change channels when I see a familiar face. The camera closes in on a woman with creamy coffee skin, short dark hair, and clear green eyes.

I don't believe it. It's Phoebe Fitz, my speed skating idol. Doing ballet. She and her partner spin side by side over and over. She looks like she's having fun. The audience loves her.

After the dance, a man in a tuxedo talks to her. "Wonderful job, Phoebe—but ballet must be quite different from speed skating, right?"

"They're not as different as you'd think. Ballet's about balance and rhythm and timing. You gotta be strong, and you gotta be fast. I'm going to make the kids I coach take it."

I flip off the TV and sit on the edge of my bed, stunned.

Well, okay. If Phoebe Fitz thinks I should do ballet, I will. I won't give up. I will give the Sugar Plum thing my very best shot.

But I'm going to need lots of help.

Chapter 12

I get to ballet class early on Saturday. Terrel's stretching, her leg propped up on the trash can. Epatha is lying on a bench admiring the shiny pink heart stickers on her fingernails. Brenda has another 5,000-page book of body parts on her lap.

I walk over to them. Epatha sits up. Terrel stops stretching. Brenda closes the book, sticking her finger in it to keep her place.

I take a deep breath. "I'm sorry I yelled at you guys. I was mad. My mom is not dating Mr. Lester. And I did not want to get that part. But I got it anyway. And I am terrible."

Terrel nods in agreement. "You *are* terrible. No offense."

Epatha squirms around on the bench. "We shouldn't have gotten mad at you, I guess. You got the part fair and square. Mr. Lester wouldn't have rigged the drawing."

I go on. "You guys are the best dancers in the class."

Epatha puffs out her cheeks and smiles a little.

"I'm not," says Brenda. "JoAnn's better than I am."

"You're still good," I say quickly. "And you're really smart. I need you all to help me learn my dance so I don't wreck the whole show. Please?"

They're quiet for a minute. My heart pounds in my chest.

"Well . . ." Epatha says. She looks at Terrel and Brenda. They nod.

"We'd have to practice outside of class," Epatha says. "Where do you live?"

I tell her.

"That's around the corner from me," she says. "And Terrel is down the street. There's a storage room in the back of our restaurant we can practice in. Everyone, come over tomorrow afternoon, okay?"

The lump in my stomach dissolves. "Thanks," I say.

The next afternoon Mama drops me off at Bella Italia, the restaurant Epatha's family owns. Epatha leads me past crowded red booths and through the noisy kitchen into a back room. Huge cans of tomato sauce and boxes of pasta line the shelves on one wall. The smell of warm lasagna and garlic bread leaks under the door and tickles my nose.

Terrel comes in carrying a boom box and a CD. "The triplets' dad had the Sugar Plum Fairy music. I borrowed it," she says.

Brenda arrives with a stack of books. This time the books aren't about blood vessels or bones; they're about ballet.

Terrel calls us to attention. "Alexandrea has three problems. She can't do spins. She does not dance with feeling and emotion. And—"

I interrupt. "How can I dance with feeling and emotion if I can't do the steps?"

"Exactly," Terrel continues. "And she does not know the steps."

"Muchos problemas," Epatha says to me. "That's a lot of problems, girl."

I already *know* all this. "So, how are we going to fix them?" I ask Terrel, trying not to whine.

"I know all the steps from watching Mr. Lester try to teach you," Terrel says. "I'll help you learn them. Epatha dances with lots of feeling. She'll help you with that. And Brenda will figure out why you can't do turns."

I'm impressed. Terrel is like a military commander going into battle. I start to feel like it might not be hopeless after all.

"Brenda, you're first," Terrel says.

Brenda looks up from the book she's reading. "Right. Spins," she says. "Watch I'll. Turn chaîné one do, Al. Okay."

I think she's telling me to do a chaîné turn. I stand with my arms out to my sides. I step across with one leg, turn my body around, and end up a few feet away.

Brenda squints and refers back to her book. "Bad not actually is technique your," she begins.

Terrel interrupts. "Brenda, talk forward so she can understand you. We've got enough problems."

Brenda sighs, as if talking forward for five minutes is going to ruin her mental development. "Okay. Your technique is actually not bad. Use your arms more, though. They'll help pull you around."

It's nice to understand Brenda for a change. I try again.

"Are you really spotting?" she asks.

"I can't," I say. "I just don't get it."

"You can't just look at the whole wall. You need to focus *really hard* on one little place. Or one thing, like . . ." She looks around. She picks up a bright red jar of marinated mushrooms and holds it in the air. "Look at the mushrooms," she says. "No, look at this *one* mushroom." She points to one mushroom smashed up against the glass of the jar.

I do.

"Now, slowly do a turn," Brenda continues. "Keep looking at the mushroom as long as you can."

I stare hard at the mushrooms. I turn my body. At the last minute, I whip my head around and look at the can again.

"Now, faster," Brenda says.

I turn once, twice, three times, my eyes burning into the can. I crash into a crate of macaroni at the end of the room. But only because I wasn't looking where I was going, not because I felt dizzy.

"You dizzy?" Brenda asks.

I push myself upright and shake my head to check. "No!" I say. "I'm not!"

We practice until I can turn without knocking over any pasta boxes.

"*Brava, bellissima!*" Epatha calls. She comes over and high-fives me. "Nice work, Brenda," she says, high-fiving her, too. Brenda smiles modestly.

"One problem down," Terrel says. "Two to go."

Chapter 13

We meet at the restaurant almost every day. Sometimes Terrel and one of her brothers pick me up, and sometimes Mama walks me over. One day a man stops Mama on the street and asks where the Apollo Theater is. I tell him before Mama can even open her mouth.

"You're turning into a real New Yorker!" she says afterward. I can tell she's proud of me.

In the restaurant storage room, Terrel works with me on my steps. She teaches me a tiny little part of the dance and makes me do it again and again. Then she hooks it up to the little tiny part that comes before, and we practice it all together.

Brenda drills me on my turns. Every day she holds up a different food package for me to stare at as I spin around. "We don't want you to get conditioned so you can only spin if you're looking at marinated mushrooms," she explains. So I do tortellini twirls, spaghetti spins, and rigatoni rotations.

Once I have the steps, Epatha helps me put some personality into them. Instead of a chassé, she does a chassé with attitude. I try to copy her.

"Don't do it like me," she says. "You gotta do it like *you*. Find your inner Sugar Plum Fairy."

What *is* a Sugar Plum Fairy, anyway? I decide she must be kind of like the tooth fairy. I close my eyes and imagine I *am* the Sugar Plum Fairy. I'm beautiful. I live in a castle. I toss candy bars onto kids' pillows while they sleep. Maybe the tooth fairy follows behind me to collect the teeth the kids lose in caramel bars.

"Now you're getting it," Epatha says with satisfaction. "You ain't just doing the steps. You're dancing."

She and Brenda and Terrel do the dance with me. Epatha stands on my left, and Terrel and Brenda on my right. When we're dancing together, I don't get nervous. I don't forget the steps. It's actually . . . I can't believe it . . . *fun*.

Mr. Lester is astonished at my progress. "Wonderful work, Alexandrea!" he calls out in the middle of my dance. I still forget the steps sometimes, but Terrel watches from the sidelines and gives me little hints or points me in the right direction.

Epatha, Brenda, Terrel, and I hang out at the restaurant all the time. Epatha's parents are cool. Instead of sticking their noses into the storage room every two seconds the way some parents would, they leave us alone. When we're done, we sit in one of the booths in the back. Nonna—Epatha's squat Italian grandma, who always wears a black dress, a white apron, and black knee-high stockings—brings over big plates of spaghetti for us.

"Much better than Puerto Rican food," she says, glaring across the room at Abuela, Epatha's other grandma.

"Mm-hmmm," says Epatha.

Tall, elegant Abuela—Epatha's Puerto Rican grandma—makes us flan; little mounds of custard with caramel on top. "Much better than Italian food," she says, winking at us.

"You bet," says Epatha. The rest of us just smile and eat everything up.

The triplets come over sometimes to practice the Monster Ballet with Epatha, Brenda, and Terrel. Then they hang out to watch my dance. They've started to pick up the steps, too, even Jerzey Mae.

Sometimes when there are no customers, the waiters come into the back to watch us. If I notice them watching, my stomach fills up with butterflies, and I freeze. I can't remember any of the steps.

After this happens for the third time, Terrel sighs. "I think we got a fourth problem," she says. "Stage fright." She looks at Brenda.

"It on I'm," Brenda says.

Brenda and Terrel come into the Nutcracker School the next day smiling. "Underwear," Brenda says.

"What?" Epatha asks.

"The solution to Al's problem," says Terrel.

"I already *wear* underwear," I say defensively.

They sit down on the bench with us. "Al has to think about underwear," says Terrel.

Brenda holds up a book called *Stop Stage Fright*.

Epatha whistles. "*Un libro para todo.* Girl, you find a book for everything."

Brenda opens the book, holds it under my nose, and points to a spot. I read out loud, *"One way to cure stage fright is to pretend everyone in the audience is sitting there in their underwear. It is quite difficult to be scared of people in underwear."*

"They ain't seen Nonna in her zebra-stripe

slip," Epatha says. "Now, *that's* scary."

But I have to admit that the underwear trick is worth a shot.

The next time the waiters watch us dance, I imagine fat old Alfredo standing there in red long underwear. I picture Fabio, who has a long mustache and is always flirting with lady customers, in shiny pink boxer shorts with hearts on them.

It works! I can hardly dance, because I'm laughing so hard, but I don't forget any of the steps.

"Underwear," I tell the other girls. They look at Alfredo and Fabio. We all crack up.

"*Ragazze pazze*—crazy girls. Always giggling over nothing." Fabio throws his hands in the air.

Epatha's mom comes in, brushing the flour off her hands. Her apron has bright green parrots on it, and her dark, wavy hair is clipped back with a shiny pink, green, and orange clip. You can tell where Epatha gets her style.

"Girls, the restaurant inspector is coming next Friday," she says. "We want to get this room cleaned up. I'm sorry, but you'll need to find somewhere else to practice next week."

"We can't do it at my house," Terrel says. "My brothers would get in the way." She has five older brothers, which is probably why she's so good at bossing people around.

"Place my to come can you," Brenda says.

"Her apartment?" I ask.

Epatha nods. "It's kind of small, but we can dance small."

We all say good-bye in the front of the restaurant. Mama lets me walk home alone from Epatha's, since it's just a block from our apartment. The air is crisp, and the late afternoon sun is turning the sky orange. I crunch through a pile of dead leaves on the sidewalk. Someone's eating fried chicken and waffles in a booth by the window of the soul food restaurant. You don't find chicken and waffles in Apple Creek, that's for sure.

All the street noise that used to keep me awake at night and make me jittery during the day seems exciting now. All these people going all these places. I pass the old guys playing checkers on the corner, as always. One of them smiles at me and tips his hat. I wave.

I walk up the creaky stairs to our apartment. I'm not even scared of them the way I used to be. But I am scared of what I see when I open our door.

Moving boxes.

Chapter 14

Mama comes out of her workroom when she hears the door creak open. Her eyes are puffy. She follows my gaze to the moving boxes stacked against the living room wall.

"I think we may need to go back to Georgia after all, Alexandrea."

"What do you mean, go back?" I ask. "We've only been here two months."

But I know that except for the dresses she made for that guy, she hasn't found any other costume jobs, even though she's been going around to lots of theaters and dance places. She says you need personal connections, which means people you know making their friends hire you.

"You can't just give up!" I tell her. "You told me not to give up on ballet. You said we had lots of potential here."

She sits down on the couch and pats the place beside her. I sit down. When we first moved here, I never thought this apartment would feel like home. But now it does. This couch fits perfectly under the windows. The ceramic handprint I made in kindergarten is hanging on the wall. I've even gotten used to my ballet-nightmare room.

"I want to be straight with you, Alexandrea. I thought I'd planned everything out, but I didn't realize how expensive New York is. And I'd hoped the business would take off faster."

She brushes my hair out of my eyes. "Fact is, it hasn't. And I don't know what else to do."

"But, Mama . . . can't you get some other kind of job for a while? Our ballet show's in two weeks—we don't have to go before then, do we?"

"If we have to move, I want to get you back

before school starts. And you know no one's bought my shop in Apple Creek yet, so I can get it back." The light seems to go out of her eyes as she says this. "But you'll be with your old friends again—that'll be nice, won't it?"

I think about Keisha and my other friends from Apple Creek. I miss them, kind of, but my life there seems as if it happened a long time ago.

Then I think about Epatha talking in three languages at once. And Terrel ordering us around. And Brenda, who can find anything anyone needs in a book. And the way they've all helped me learn my dance.

"Mama, I really want to stay now. Please?"

She looks at me for a long time. "We'll stay till your show's done. After that, unless something changes . . ."

She doesn't need to finish her sentence. I stuff the moving boxes back into the closet and give them a good hard kick.

Chapter 15

On Sunday afternoon, Terrel's big brother, Cheng, takes us to the park. He has some really old roller skates that fit Terrel if she sticks cotton in the toes, so I told her I'd teach her to skate. Cheng hangs out on a bench with his friends while I show Terrel how to lace up the skates just right. After all the time she spent going over the dance with me, it feels good that I can finally show her something.

Terrel stands up. The right skate starts wheeling right, and the left one starts wheeling left. I grab her before she falls on her rear—good thing her brother has a helmet we can use, too.

"I guess this is how you felt when you were

learning the Sugar Plum dance," she pants, after falling over for the fifth time.

When she's had enough skating for the day, it's my turn. I tie on the skates. They're a perfect fit. Terrel sits on a bench while I race up and down the sidewalk. I see an older lady wearing a huge feathered hat on the sidewalk across the street.

"That's the lady who picks you up after class sometimes, right?" I ask Terrel.

Terrel nods. "It's my grandma. She must be coming back from church."

"That's quite a hat," I say.

"All the ladies at her church wear big hats," Terrel replies. "They call them crowns. It's like they try to out-hat each other. Grandma has at least twenty of them, and she buys more whenever she goes to a church convention."

It feels like puzzle pieces are floating around in my brain but they're not fitting together yet.

"Where does she buy them?" I ask.

"She used to get them at a place called Emma's Crowns, but Emma got old and went to Florida. Grandma says there're no really good hat shops around anymore."

The puzzle pieces snap into place.

"Let's meet at my apartment on Monday instead of Brenda's," I say. "And have your grandma come pick you up after."

"Why?" Terrel asks.

"You'll see."

Chapter 16

On Monday afternoon, Mama runs down to the store to get snacks for us to have after we practice. While she's gone, I move all the hats she's made from the workroom out to the living room. I set them on their hat stands, too, so it looks like a bunch of fancy, faceless ladies are perched around the edge of the room.

"What are all my hats doing out?" Mama asks, as she shuts the door and puts away her handbag.

I think fast. "We need an audience so it feels more like we're performing."

"Well, don't knock them over," she says.

All the girls show up at our apartment at

the same time. I introduce Mama to everyone.

"Wow—you look like a model," Epatha says. "What a cool outfit."

Cool is right—it's the Iceberg Suit. My friends all walk around Mama and admire the shimmering fabric.

"I wish my mom had a suit like that," Brenda says.

Mama brushes off their compliments, but I can tell she's pleased.

"Can I watch you ladies practice?" she asks me.

I get nervous thinking about her watching, and I do not want to have to picture my Mama in underwear. "No—I want it to be a surprise," I tell her.

After we go through my dance, and then the Monster Dance for good measure, we have some cookies and juice. Then Epatha asks if we can see Mama's workroom.

"Sure," I tell her.

We go back, and Epatha heads straight to the costume rack. "Wow," she says. "Wow, wow, wow." She goes right to an orange dress with feathers and a matching headpiece. "This is totally me."

Mama smiles. "Let's see how it looks." She takes the dress, leads Epatha to the mirror, and holds it in front of her. "I think you're right—that dress *is* you."

Meanwhile, Brenda is looking with interest at the drawers of sequins.

"You make all those hats out front?" Terrel asks Mama.

"Yes," Mama says. "I mostly do costumes, but I like hats, too."

Terrel gives me a big grin. "Now I know why you wanted to practice over here," she whispers.

Epatha calls me over to admire her. Pretty soon we're all parading around the room in different costumes and hats. Mama even talks Brenda into trying on a black-and-white dress with a big, triangle-shaped collar.

"Up-dress playing of think would Vinci da Leonardo what know don't I," says Brenda.

"*What* did she say?" Mama whispers to Terrel.

"She says she doesn't know what Leonardo da Vinci would think of playing dress-up," Terrel tells Mama.

"Well, he's been dead for about a million years, so we ain't gonna tell him," says Epatha.

The doorbell rings. Mama calls down on the intercom. "Who is it?"

"Mahalia Ducket, Terrel's grandma," a voice crackles through the speaker.

Mama buzzes her up.

The door opens, and Mrs. Ducket comes in. She's tiny with dark brown skin, like

Terrel. She has crooked teeth, like Terrel. She marches right over to one of the hat stands, moving exactly like a bigger version of Terrel.

"My goodness," she says. "Where did these lovely hats come from?"

"My mama makes them," I say. "She sells them, too."

Mrs. Ducket goes from hat stand to hat stand. She picks up some of the hats. We all watch in silence. Mama looks as if she can't quite figure out what's happening.

"May I try these on?" Mrs. Ducket asks.

"Uh . . . of course," Mama says. "I'll get you a mirror."

Mrs. Ducket tries on a pink hat with netting and a huge cloth hydrangea on top. She tries on a black hat with squares of silver netting that dangle down. She tries on the orange and purple hat that looks like an ostrich's rear end.

"I'll take them," she says.

"Which?" Mama asks, a little dazed.

"All three," Mrs. Ducket says. "The ladies at my church wear fancy hats. We buy *lots* of hats. And these are one-of-a-kind. How much?"

Mama pauses. I don't know if she's even thought about how much to charge.

Mrs. Ducket opens her purse, takes out a stack of bills, and hands them to Mama. "Okay?"

Mama's eyes get big. She nods.

"I'll pick them up tomorrow," says Mrs. Ducket. "Can you make more? If you can, I'll bring some of my friends by. But let me tell you something," she says, leaning closer to Mama. "You should charge them twice as much. These hats are worth it." She winks, turns briskly, and marches out the door.

Mama throws her arms around Terrel. "Your grandma may have just saved our skins." She looks at me. "You put those hats out there to be an audience, did you?"

"Yes, ma'am," I say, grinning. She gives me a big hug, too, and twirls me around in the air.

The doorbell rings. Mrs. Ducket comes back upstairs.

"Did you forget something?" Mama asks.

"Yes," Mrs. Ducket says. She takes Terrel by the hand and pulls her out the door.

Chapter 17

Before we know it, it's the weekend before the show.

Ballet One, Ballet Two, and Ballet Three classes all share one program, so everyone from kindergartners to fourth graders comes to the ballet school on Saturday to get costumes. One studio has been turned into a costume room. Mama volunteered to help out (which is why the giraffe is chocolate brown with shimmering gold spots and the elephant wears an exotic hat). A few other harried moms measure kids and pull costumes off the racks for them. They also sew the costumes back together when the kids wreck them, which is usually about two minutes after they put them on.

"Kitties, hold your tails up!" one of the moms yells. "And try not to step on them!" A circle of tailless cats surround her, waving tails that need to be sewn back on. The Ballet Two teacher finally decides the cats will be Manx cats.

On the other side of the room, Tiara Girl is struggling to get into her warthog suit. She has to wear a big papier-mâché warthog head with bristly ears and big tusks. I wonder if they make warthog-size tiaras. I smile and wave at her. She glowers back.

Epatha, Brenda, Terrel, and the triplets get their furry monster costumes. The costumes look even more like hairy grapes in person than they did in the drawing. Jerzey Mae looks miserable. She sidles over to the rack where my fairy costume is hanging and runs a finger gently along a row of sequins.

"You want to try it on?" I ask. I help her into it. "The Monster Ballet is really cute," I say, as she admires herself in the mirror.

"At least no one can see it's me inside the suit," she says.

Mama's racing around like crazy, pinning and sewing. She's on her knees adjusting the giraffe's tail when I see Mr. Lester and Ms. Debbé come in. Mr. Lester leads Ms. Debbé over to Mama and taps Mama on the back.

"Mom, I'd like you to meet Yolanda Johnson. She's been doing a great job for us making some new costumes and reworking the old ones."

Mama's eyes get big as Ms. Debbé extends her hand. For a minute I'm afraid Mama might kiss it, like someone would kiss a king's hand in an old movie. But Mama pulls herself together and shakes Ms. Debbé's hand.

"The costumes, they look simply wonderful," Ms. Debbé says. "You have much talent."

Mama looks like she's about to pass out.

"Ms. Johnson is starting a costume business," Mr. Lester says.

"Really?" says Ms. Debbé. "Please see that I get some of your business cards. I will tell my friends about you."

Ms. Debbé sweeps out of the room. Mr. Lester follows her. On his way out, he gives me a wink.

Mama, for the first time in her life, is totally speechless.

The show's set for next Saturday night. On Friday afternoon, we have a dress rehearsal up in the big studio. It looks like a real theater. There's a stage at one end, with big red and black curtains on the side. There are lots of chairs set up for the audience. A guy stands on a ladder messing with some spotlights.

"No luck," he says to Ms. Debbé, who is hovering next to him. "The circuit's not working."

"We must have lights for the show!" Ms. Debbé says. "It is essential!"

"Don't worry, you'll have your lights," he says. One of the dancing cats chases another, then clobbers her, nearly knocking over the ladder.

"I'll come back after all these . . . uh, precious little girls are gone," the lighting guy says.

Meanwhile, Mr. Lester tries to organize the Ballet Three girls while two of the other teachers wrangle the littler kids. "Monsters over here! Animals there! Raindrops, by the back wall!"

He tells us we'll wait quietly—he emphasizes *quietly*—in the studio across the hall till he comes to get each group. We'll stand backstage until the applause for the previous number finishes; then we'll go on and do our dances.

"All except you, Al," he says. "You'll be

right after intermission. The monsters will wait backstage for your dance to end."

"Quiet, everyone!" Ms. Debbé raps her walking stick for attention. "Our dress rehearsal is beginning!"

We get to sit and watch the little kids dance, since we won't be able to see them tomorrow.

I sit between Brenda and Epatha in the third row. The Ballet One kids are all dressed like little yellow flowers. Their teacher dances with them, but one flower still wanders off the stage in the middle of the dance. Another sits down in the center of the stage and starts bawling. One starts singing, *"Row, row, row your boat,"* at the top of her lungs. When we laugh, she looks pleased and sings even louder. The teacher smiles as if she couldn't be happier that these kids are wrecking her dance. Mr. Lester finally comes on, scoops up the singer and the crier, and carries them offstage.

Some of the Ballet Two girls are doing a princess dance. They all have pink, fluffy dresses and crowns.

"Everyone gets to look nice except us," I hear Jerzey Mae whisper behind me.

"Maybe you'll get to be a princess next year," Jessica says soothingly.

"Princess, shmincess," JoAnn says. "Why can't we do a skateboard dance?"

We watch the princesses, then the dancing tailless cats. After their dance ends, Mr. Lester leads all the Ballet Three girls out of the audience and across the hall. "Animals and raindrops, stay here," he says. "Alexandrea, you and the monsters follow me."

We go back into the studio by a side door so we're hidden from the audience. I hear the little kids thumping into the seats to watch us.

"Monsters, wait backstage—you can watch Alexandrea's dance from the wings. When it's almost over, prepare to come on. Alexandrea, take your place in the center of the stage. The curtain will open. When you're ready, look at me and I'll start the music."

I go to the middle of the stage. It feels lonely and big. I stretch my arms out like I'm supposed to. I hear ropes creaking, and the curtain opens slowly. My stomach flutters.

Suddenly I'm looking out on the roomful of kids. There are millions of them. My mind goes blank. What am I doing up here? I can't remember the first step. I can't even remember my own name!

"Psst!" Brenda whispers from the wings. "Underwear!"

I look out and choose a girl in the front row. I imagine her in underwear instead of her yellow flower outfit. She's not so scary. I imagine rows and rows of kids in goofy underwear.

Chassé left! That's the first step. I nod to Mr. Lester. He starts the music.

My dance goes just fine after that. When I'm done, I curtsy the way Mr. Lester showed me, then go off to the wings to watch the monsters. Even Jerzey Mae does well.

When they come off, Epatha gives me a hug. "Nice work, Sugar Plum Fairy," she says.

"Nice work, monsters," I reply.

Ms. Debbé comes backstage and kisses both of my cheeks. "*Fantastique!* You see? All students have potential. It was easy, yes?"

Epatha, Terrel, Brenda, and I exchange looks.

"It was easy, no," I say.

"Tomorrow will be a piece of cake," Mr. Lester says. "That's why we have dress rehearsals like this—so there won't be any surprises the night of the show."

But Mr. Lester is wrong.

Chapter 18

"Hurry up, Mama," I say. She's been messing with my hair forever. "We gotta get there by seven o'clock."

"I know when we gotta get there, Miss Sugar Plum Fairy," she says, putting another little white sparkly flower into my hair. "Almost done."

After three more snaps, she steps back to admire her work. She turns me around to face the mirror. "Does your mama rock, or what?"

The top of my white dress sparkles with all the new sequins Mama has added. Layer after airy layer of fabric floats around my hips. My hair is slicked back in a bun, with the flowers all over catching the light when I move.

"Yes, ma'am. You definitely rock," I reply.

"Nervous?" she asks.

"Why would I be nervous?" I ask. No need to be nervous when I have the underwear trick ready to go.

"That's right, baby," she says. "You all have been practicing so much that you can probably do that dance in your sleep."

She's right—I did the dance over and over in my dreams last night. Every step was right on. Nothing can go wrong now.

"Come on, Alexandrea—let's go get a cab," Mama says.

"A cab?" I say as she opens the door.

"Dance stars do *not* walk to the theater when they perform," she says. She waves her arm in the air when we get outside, and a taxi pulls right up in front of us.

I've never been in a cab before. I sit in the back with Mama. We race through traffic and get to the dance studio in no time at all. Mama hands the driver some money, then gives me a hug.

"Break a leg, baby," she says.

"What?" I shriek. That seems like a rotten thing to say to your daughter when she's about to do a dance.

She laughs. "It's theater talk. Show people think it's bad luck to say, 'good luck,' so they say, 'break a leg' instead."

"Oh." I walk up the stairs very carefully anyway.

After Mama goes to get a seat, I go to the studio where the Ballet Three girls are supposed to meet. Mr. Lester checks my name off his list. All the monsters are already here. Epatha waves me over. She grins at me through the face hole in her purple monster costume. Even her cheeks are purple.

"If you're going to be purple, you might as well be *all* purple," she says. "I used some of my mom's eye shadow."

"How long before we go on?" I ask.

"Minutes twenty about take dances kids' little the," says Brenda.

I'm too nervous even to try to figure that one out. I look at Terrel.

"If the little kids take twenty minutes, we're probably on at eight," she says.

A whole hour.

"You guys scared?" I ask.

"Naaah," says Epatha.

Brenda raises her eyebrow. Epatha's foot is tapping as if she's trying to talk in Morse code.

"Well . . . a little," Epatha admits.

Soon we hear a burst of applause. The show must be starting. We can hear the flower dance music leaking under the door.

"Let's sneak out and see how many people are there," Epatha says.

Brenda, Terrel, and I follow her into the hallway. The door to the big studio is open a crack. Epatha peeks in.

"*Mamma mia,*" she says. "That's one heck of a lot of people."

I look inside. The studio is totally jammed. Every single seat is filled. People are standing at the back and along the sides. There are even people sitting on the floor right in front of the stage. We overhear two of the moms talking to each other. "I counted over two hundred people—isn't that wonderful?" one of them says.

We walk silently back to the room.

"I didn't know there would be *that* many," Terrel says.

Now that I know how many people are out there, I decide I can wait a while to do my dance. In fact, I can wait forever.

But before we know it, it's intermission, and Mr. Lester is leading the monsters and me down the hallway.

"You'll all be wonderful, girls," he says reassuringly. I swallow hard. Maybe there will be a fire drill, and they'll stop the show. Maybe a UFO will crash into the roof. Maybe . . .

"Alexandrea, you're on," he says. I don't move. He takes me by the shoulders and pushes me toward the stage. I can see the monsters lined up in the wings.

I stretch my arms out. Underwear, I think to myself. Underwear, underwear, underwear.

The ropes squeak, and the curtains part. A bright light hits me in the face like a fist. They got the lights fixed—but they're blinding me. I can't see out into the audience.

Applause fills the room. They're clapping for me. My stomach flips and flops. My mind goes blank. I can't remember anything except underwear.

How can I picture someone in underwear if I can't see the audience at all? I squint to try to make out a face, but all I see are blobs of black and the fierce shine of the lights pointing onstage. I start to panic.

I continue to stand there with my arms out. The audience stops clapping and waits expectantly.

I stand.

And stand.

Mr. Lester waits for me to look at him so he can start the music.

I will never remember the steps. I will be standing here onstage with everyone staring at me for the rest of my life. A drop of sweat rolls down the side of my face.

Then, out of the corner of my eye, I see something move. Something purple.

Epatha walks onstage. She plants herself to my left, just like she did when we practiced the dance together.

Terrel and Brenda come onstage, too. They stand on my right.

Even the triplets come on. They stand behind us.

Epatha nods to Mr. Lester. His eyes look a

little wild, but he starts the music.

"Let's do it, girlfriend," Epatha says.

The steps flood back into my head as the music starts. We chassé left, then right. It's just like all the times we practiced in the restaurant. I can almost smell the lasagna.

With my friends beside me, I jump like a gazelle and even spin, spin, spin like a real ballerina. The triplets do the dance, too, even though Jerzey Mae goes left one time she's supposed to go right. But it doesn't matter.

When we finish, the room explodes with applause. We line up, all together, and curtsy. *"Thank you,"* I whisper to all of my friends as I leave the stage. Epatha winks. Then they get into place for their dance.

After the show is over, we push our way past all the parents and friends back to our dressing room. We're behind a well-dressed man and lady. The lady says, "I loved the Sugar Plum Fairy's dance. But what were those purple things?"

"Those were the Sugar Plums," the man replies knowingly.

Epatha nudges me.

Mama comes in with Terrel's grandma and dad, Epatha's parents, Brenda's mom, and the triplets' mom and dad. They hug us all and tell us how great we were.

Mr. Lester appears while we're pulling on our jackets. "Not exactly what we'd planned, but very nice, girls. How did your friends learn your dance, Alexandrea?"

"We aren't just her friends," Epatha says. "We're her sisters."

"We are the Sugar Plum Sisters," says Terrel. She locks pinkies with Epatha, who locks them with Brenda, who locks them with JoAnn, who locks them with Jerzey Mae, who locks them with Jessica, who locks them with me.

"Sugar Plum Power!" Epatha says.

"Sugar Plum Power!" we all say.

Then we walk with our families out into the cool night air toward Bella Italia, where six extralarge pizzas are waiting for us.

Chapter 19

It's September eighth, my birthday, and we're down at the Chelsea Piers skating rink for my birthday party. Finally I'm gliding over the ice. My skates fly as I go around and around and around the rink.

"You're really good!" JoAnn says. "You should try skateboarding."

Mama gives her a look. "She should *not* try skateboarding."

Brenda nods. I hear her say, "Ice-skating is safer. When you fall, there's less friction. That means you glide instead of getting all ripped up. Although I did just read about how to sew people up with stitches."

"What did she say?" Mama asks, bewildered.

I stare at Brenda. "Did you say that forward or backward?"

She looks at me like I'm crazy. "Backward."

I can't believe it! I can finally understand Brenda. I grin so hard my cheeks hurt.

A lot's happened since the show. Mrs. Ducket showed off her hats to her friends, who told their friends. Mama's set up a hat shop next door to Aunt Jackie's hair salon. It's called Yolanda's Crowns for Urban Royalty. Mama can't make hats fast enough to keep up with business. She's even getting some costume jobs from friends of Ms. Debbé. That means we get to stay here. And I'm glad.

Mama smiles as I zoom around the rink. The triplets have never skated in their lives. JoAnn gets it fast, but Jerzey Mae and Jessica are clutching each other. Epatha's a natural, and Terrel's doing okay, too—I think the roller-skating might have helped.

I go to the edge for a breather. Mama comes over.

"You look really happy, birthday girl," she says.

"I am." I smile at her.

"I haven't forgotten our deal, Alexandrea. If you want to quit ballet and take skating, you can."

I look at my friends out on the ice. JoAnn's trying to spin. Brenda's calling out encouragement to her (backward!). Terrel's struggling to pull Jerzey Mae and Jessica up from the heap they've fallen into. Epatha skates over to Mama and me.

"Can I take skating *and* ballet?" I ask.

"I think we might be able to arrange that," Mama says. She gazes into the distance, then slams her hands down on the edge of the rink.

"Why didn't I think of this before?" she says. "You can be a figure skater! That way, you can skate *and* still wear beautiful costumes!

And I know exactly what outfit to make for your first competition. I'm seeing blue— electric-sky blue . . . more lightning bolts . . . maybe some feathers, to represent birds in flight . . ."

Epatha's eyes pop out in horror. I laugh. At least it's progress.

I grab Epatha's hand and pull her away. "Race you around the rink," I say. And we're off, ice shavings flying behind us.

Al's Guide
to Ballet Terms

barre—the bar you hold on to in order to keep yourself from falling over when you're doing things like pliés.

chaîné turns—turns you do in a straight line or a circle unless you're terrible at them like I used to be. If you're like I was, you do a few, then crash into the wall.

chassé—step where you move across the floor with one foot chasing the other. It's kind of like a gallop, but gallop doesn't sound fancy enough for ballet.

first position—when your heels are together and your toes (or, as Brenda would say, your phalanges) stick out.

grand battement—big kick. If Tiara Girl's standing in front of me at the barre, I do these extra-big.

grand jeté—big leap across the floor. I'm really good at these unless my tutu falls off.

plié—knee-bend. A **demi-plié** is a little one, and a **grand plié** is a big one. Epatha adds little jumps and flashy arm moves when Ms. Debbé's not looking.

relevé—when you go up on your toes. When Terrel does this, she's almost as tall as the rest of us (unless we're doing it too; then she's out of luck).

spot—look hard at something (like a jar of marinated mushrooms) so you don't get dizzy while you're turning.